DATE			

Landscape Design Guide

Volume 1
Soft Landscape

Authors: Adrian Lisney and Ken Fieldhouse

Editor Jeremy Dodd

Gower Technical

Published by
Gower Publishing Company Limited
Gower House
Croft Road
Aldershot
Hants GU11 3HR
England

Gower Publishing Company
Old Post Road
Brookfield
Vermont 05036
USA

British Library Cataloguing in Publication Data
Adrian Lisney
   Landscape design.
   Vol. 1: Soft landscape.
   1. Landscape design
   I. Title II. Fieldhouse, Ken III. Dodd, Jeremy
   712

ISBN 0 566 09017 1

Printed in Great Britain by BPCC Wheatons Ltd, Exeter

Contents

Preface

The Department of the Environment has, over the years produced a number of landscape design guides and landscape brochures. The first was issued in 1971 and the most recent in 1988 as 'Landscape Design for the Nation'. Some, like the Housing Development Notes 'Landscape of New Housing' dealt with the broader concepts of landscape design. Others gave advice on specific landscape topics such as 'Existing Trees and Buildings' in response to the widespread desire to develop land while retaining existing trees with their many and diverse benefits to site quality.

Some years ago it was decided to bring the design guide material together in a more convenient form for the general public as well as environmental design professions and, at the same time, to update it thoroughly. It is now published in two companion volumes in which design with plants is covered by Volume 1: *Soft Landscape* and built works in the landscape covered in Volume 2: *Hard Landscape.*

The design guide firmly concentrates on principles and broad concepts, rather than going into great depth on highly specific aspects of construction or planting because there is such a broad wealth of published material available on every conceivable specialist topic. The essential facts needed to achieve good landscape design are stressed; however, to help those who want to study a single aspect of landscape design in great depth, advice on further reading is given both in the text and more broadly in the bibliography at the end of each volume.

The growing public awareness of the importance of the landscape environment is now apparent in many ways. Public concern extends beyond preserving fine individual trees to conserving the most valuable landscapes on a local as well as a national scale. They are often scenically and scientifically irreplaceable. Beyond that, it extends to development of underused land with ecological and social or recreational potential. Once vacant, land colonized by natural succession soon becomes vigorous woodland.

Naturally, it has its many defenders in the climate of today's growing environmental consciousness. Now bleak city areas that stemmed from a combination of ill-considered urban design when rebuilding was taking place in the 1950s and 60s and which lack adequate urban landscape provision need to be tackled. Many parks too are no longer attractive because of their open and windswept character. To remedy many of these conditions it is insufficient merely to plant attractive trees and shrubs to hide the defects; it is necessary to follow a more functionally inspired approach through the art and science of landscape planning. For example, shelter planting designed to save energy, to reduce noise and to reduce air pollution can, when used coherently on a city scale, improve living and working conditions. The success of these measures can be observed in towns and cities that once again attract people.

PSA's consultant authors, Adrian Lisney and Ken Fieldhouse, Landscape Architects, in association with the general editor Jeremy Dodd, have been responsible for the text, many sketches and excellent photography. Studies by several landscape consultants including work by Maurice Pickering and the late Clifford Tandy have been incorporated.

MICHAEL ELLISON

Chief Landscape Architect

P.S.A (D.o.E)

February 1990

Acknowledgements

Adrian Lisney and Ken Fieldhouse gratefully acknowledge the particular assistance of Penny Anderson: *Plant Ecology* section; Ray Adams: *Agriculture and Horticulture*; Simon Bell: *Forestry*; Nicholas Simpson, Comtec UK Ltd., *Hydraulic Seeding*; Robin Voelcker, Dr Augustus Voelcker & Sons Ltd., *Soils;* and more generally Rosalyn Guard; Anne Lankaster; and Michael Oldham.

We would like to thank the many individual photographers and Michael Oldham for all the sketches and diagrams. We would also like to acknowledge Christine Smith and Sheila Harvey's assistance with the Bibliography and Sarah Oram's unstinting efforts in typing the numerous manuscripts.

Tim Jemison of the PSA contributed to the photographic content.

CHAPTER 1

Introduction

This volume appraises the principles of planting design, and includes practical comments on plant selection and planting techniques.

The fundamental importance of planting design as an aspect of landscape architecture cannot be overemphasized. In order to achieve the best results, the designer draws inspiration from the character of the site, including groups of trees, buildings and the spaces they enclose – the *genius loci*. The shape of the ground's surface, the sunny slopes, the hollows and high places, the way the rainfall is blown across the site, the impact of cold winter winds and the nature of the plants which thrive there, can together inspire a good response to a well prepared design brief.

The fact that no two sites are identical, is a most important feature of landscape architecture and it is therefore essential to carry out a thorough visual and physical survey of every site before design work begins. Moreover, no two people are likely to have comparable requirements or expectations of their sites. Each scheme should be designed to meet the client's brief, taking account of the physical conditions of the site and the designer's subjective assessment of its character and surroundings. All too often the landscape is added as an afterthought or a cosmetic finish. The importance of the landscape potential of a site and the proper siting of buildings should be considered *together* at the outset of any proposed development.

The following basic principles should be considered in relation to the client's brief and the site character.

1. Apply a unified approach to the development as a whole. The development of land generally should be an integrated process in which the client, landscape architect, town planner, architect, civil and services engineers collaborate from the outset.
2. Begin the design process with a thorough site survey and analysis to establish the physical characteristics of the site, the opportunities it offers as well as the constraints it imposes on design.
3. Incorporate an appropriate design philosophy. For example, principles such as unity and simplicity can help to create effective and practical solutions as well as providing continuity throughout a scheme. Is it important for the design to be well integrated with the character of the locality in terms of scale, landform and plants, or are there compelling reasons for creating a contrast with the setting?
4. Carefully select plant materials appropriate to the site and to the design concept.
5. Consider how best to achieve the design philosophy within the project budget.

6. Apply conservation principles wherever appropriate. For example, rural planting schemes often centre on the preservation of a nucleus of existing trees following strong public demand. The traditional patterns of hedges, trees and woodlands are treasured for their aesthetic, historical and ecological values. There may also be a justifiable case backed by public pressure to retain areas free of *all* development, to allow the existing vegetation and wildlife to continue to flourish.

7. Assess the need for public consultation. It may be an important part of the design process on a particular project. When the opportunity arises, the designers should communicate with the people who are affected by a proposed development, including adjoining landowners.

   The active interest and involvement of local children can frequently help the long-term success of planting schemes, encourage an understanding of the value of natural vegetation and the wildlife that it supports. The support of the general public, as well as those directly involved, can help a scheme to be respected and help to reduce vandalism.

8. Consider carefully the effects of time because landscape is essentially dynamic. A planting scheme changes progressively over time, from the initial stages, until it becomes established and mature.

9. Consider future management objectives. Consult, if possible, those responsible for the future landscape management of a project.

   Because maintenance techniques have a marked influence on a design's development, the resources available for maintenance and management should be considered at an early stage. Where maintenance costs are high they are a constant drain on resources. Today emphasis is increasingly being placed upon low-maintenance designs and this is an important consideration. Although the initial establishment costs of low-maintenance schemes may be high, long-term cost benefits generally more than offset this.

This volume provides only representative illustrations of plant types to make particular points in the text. It makes no attempt to provide a comprehensive analysis. There are many good specialist books, guides and catalogues which provide detailed descriptions and illustrations of plants, together with their characteristics and environmental requirements. No amount of description can accurately portray the substance of a plant and the character of plant groupings. A full understanding of plant material is best gained from observation and experience over the years.

CHAPTER 2

Plant Growth

Planting design requires a thorough understanding of the conditions necessary for healthy plant growth. The first essential is the ability of the plant to grow and thrive in a given position as Sylvia Crowe says in *Garden Design*. Growth depends upon a number of interrelated factors. It is sensible to choose plants which originate in climatic conditions similar to those on the site. Wind exposure, temperature variations, the amount of sun or shade, dry or moist conditions, the fertility and acidity or alkalinity of the soil (pH), all influence plant growth significantly. Pollution of the air, soil or groundwater tends to drastically modify plant growth. However, the specialized techniques for dealing with the complex problems associated with industrial reclamation sites are outside the scope of this volume.

Plants vary in their requirements for light, water and nutrients, as well as in their susceptibility to frost and wind. Although many plants can tolerate a wide range of conditions, others have distinct preferences for particular soils and climate and do not thrive elsewhere. There are a set of optimum conditions for maximum growth of every species. Perhaps surprisingly, some flower most prolifically in the poorest of soils. The best guide to what is likely to grow well in a particular place is observation of what is already growing there.

When developing a planting design, it should be borne in mind that the environment of individual plants can change as the scheme matures. This applies especially to the availability of light when, for example, trees or vigorous shrubs progressively shade out the vegetation below their expanding canopies.

Plant growth rates vary widely. Some, like yew or box, are slow, growing only 50–100mm per year, whilst others, such as willow or poplar, may grow more than a metre in a year under favourable conditions. The eventual size of a tree or shrub is influenced by its environment and by the care it receives.

Climate

Exposure

Many tender plants cannot tolerate the effects of wind and need shelter to survive, particularly where the winds are cold, dry or salt-laden. Shelter can help to extend the range of plants that can be grown on an exposed site.

To establish themselves satisfactorily in windy locations, plants need to develop root systems which are much more extensive than the above-ground shoots. Particular attention should be given to ground preparation since plants must gain a good roothold as quickly as possible after planting. For trees, staking is essential, except for very small transplants. Generally, small young plants are better able to establish following root disturbance than larger, older ones. In fact, when planting on exposed sites, pruning may be advisable to reduce the shoot-root ratio.

Frost

The frequency, severity and timing of the earliest and latest frosts varies from region to region within the British Isles. There are two main influences. The first is the proximity to warm sea currents and the second is the cooling effect of increasing height above sea level. Nevertheless, the degree of frost experienced can vary within a particular site, as the movement of cold air is influenced by the topography. Cold air flows downhill and can accumulate in hollows and behind walls and hedges across steep slopes creating frost pockets, unless positive steps can be taken to divert its flow. Temperatures can also be reduced in gaps between buildings, where locally higher wind speeds are likely to induce chilling of plants. There are also areas where frost is less likely to occur, such as in the shelter of other plants, against a south facing wall or in a courtyard.

Light

Plants use daylight to convert carbon dioxide and water to carbohydrates and oxygen by the process of photosynthesis. The intensity of light received by a plant is affected by the amount of cloud cover, air pollution, deposits on the leaves, altitude and any shading vegetation. The aspect and the degree of shading by buildings also affects the intensity of light received by a plant.

Plants differ in their light requirements. Some require full sun and can tolerate the hot, dry conditions that occur, for example, at the foot of a south-facing wall, generally due to heat reflection from the wall and the shallowness of the soil layer above the foundations. Sun-loving plants that do not receive sufficient light may survive in shade, but generally fail to flower.

Other plants thrive in shady conditions, provided that the shade is not too dense. The degree of shade can vary from the dappled shade cast by light-foliaged trees such as false acacia or birch, to the deeper shade found under laurels or horse-chestnuts. The deepest shade occurs below such plants as yew which can prevent other plants growing beneath its canopy. Being often associated with lack of water, due to competition from tree roots, deep shade is a particularly stressful situation for plants.

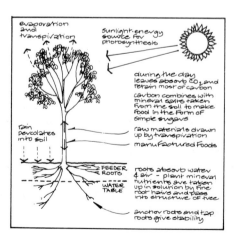

Figure 2.1   A summary of the complex processes governing plant growth.

Winter- or early spring-flowering species, such as some of the camellias and winter jasmine, cannot tolerate early morning sun on their flowers or buds which can be damaged after a frosty night. Plants such as these are best grown against a west-facing wall.

Water

Water, essential for the survival and growth of plants, is absorbed through their fine roots. All the mineral nutrients that a plant needs are taken up through the root system from the soil solution.

The amount of water available to plants depends on local precipitation and the nature of the soil. In dry weather it can be drawn up from the water table by capillary action. Deeper rooting plants are better able to survive drought conditions. Lack of water induces severe stresses which manifest themselves in wilting, particularly in the case of small plants which have little internal storage capacity.

The stresses that trees and shrubs suffer from the disturbance of being transplanted can be reduced by dipping the bare roots in a water-retentive alginate solution, or by adding peat or a water-storing polymer to the soil in which they are planted. Anti-dessicant sprays applied to the foliage can also help to reduce water stress at the time of planting if the weather is unseasonally warm.

It is necessary to ensure that there is sufficient water available throughout the establishment period. This is particularly true for semi-mature trees which may require watering for a number of years, particularly during prolonged dry spells. For amenity landscapes in Britain, a permanent irrigation system was generally thought to be uneconomic except for prestige planting schemes, roof gardens, sports facilities such as golf courses, plant nurseries and for luxury private gardens. However, as simpler, low-cost trickle irrigation systems are now available the situation is changing.

Water losses from plants can be reduced in exposed situations by the use of shelter. On light soils, water retention can also be enhanced by the addition of organic matter.

Water availability is affected by changes to the subsoil drainage pattern. On soils that have been badly compacted, drainage is poor, and excess water is often retained in clay-based soils, drowning plants. Deep cultivation to shatter the compacted zones is essential to restore sufficient porosity for air and water to permeate the soil and so encourage the root growth.

Soils

Soils normally consist of three distinct horizons, the upper topsoil layer, (the A horizon) in which feeder roots predominate, the underlying subsoil layer, (the B horizon) where anchor roots take hold, and below this the parent materials from which the mineral fractions of the soil are derived, (the C horizon).

Topsoil is a complex substance. Derived from inorganic subsoil, it incorporates complex organic materials arising from the decay of living organisms and the mineral elements essential for plant growth.

The porous 'crumb' structure of topsoil, created and maintained by the activities of soil fauna (such as worms) and stabilized by organic molecules, is very sensitive and damage to its structure should be prevented. It is vulnerable to compaction by trampling or machinery and can be contaminated by spilled chemicals or oils.

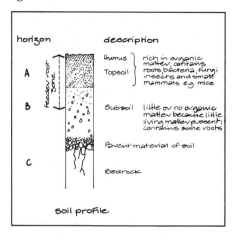

Figure 2.2   Diagrammatic soil profile –not to scale.

It is important to ensure that both the topsoil and the subsoil within areas where planting or grass is to be established are not compacted by construction machinery during building operations. If the soil does become compacted, then quite costly remedial measures such as deep ripping, ploughing or rotovating, must be carried out before planting takes place. However because of the fragile nature of topsoil, these measures are never entirely satisfactory. Therefore, all possible steps should be taken to use lightweight equipment and to restrict work on both topsoil and subsoil to times when they are dry.

Inorganic particles

Each type of underlying rock gives rise to a characteristic soil type as it becomes fragmented into small particles. In Britain, as a result of the movement of the parent materials by water, glaciers or wind, soils are sometimes unrelated to the underlying geology. The weathering of rock is primarily caused by mechanical action, chemical action or biological action.

The fine particles of soil, less than 2mm in diameter, are classified into three groups, by size. The smallest are clays (less than 0.002mm), then silts (0.002–0.05mm), and the largest are sands (0.05–2.00mm). Most soils comprise a mixture of all three and are classified into 12 descriptive classes.

The main soils types found in Britain, are described below.

Sands Sandy soils do not form a stable crumb structure, although the relatively large spaces between sand particles make them free-draining. Thus, plants growing on them are susceptible to drought and poor growth as they do not retain nutrients in solution for long. Moreover, the finer silts or sandy soils are particularly liable to erosion. Nevertheless, where there is a reliable supply of water and plant nutrients, they are an excellent growing medium.

Sufficient organic matter must be present to aid the development of a crumb structure and enhance water retention. But, as organic matter breaks down rapidly in these soils, it frequently needs to be replaced. Careful management is required to ensure that moisture stress does not become a problem.

Clay soils The structure of clay particles facilitates the retention of both moisture and nutrients although the rate of infiltration is low. However, most clay soils become sticky, unworkable and liable to compaction when wet. When clay soils dry out in hot weather they become hard and shrink, causing large surface cracks. In winter they are liable to swell. Although clays are potentially rich soils because of their high mineral content, thorough cultivation is required to improve the soil structure where it has not previously been cultivated. Rough cultivation is best during the autumn, leaving the cloddy soil over the winter to weather and be broken down by frost. The addition of suitable quantities of lime and organic materials can improve both structure and fertility.

Chalk soils Chalk soils are light, often shallow, alkaline and of low fertility. Because the underlying chalk is free-draining, plants grown on them may be vulnerable to drought. The degree of alkalinity controls the range of plants that can thrive on them. They benefit from the addition of organic matter which improves both fertility and water retention.

Loams Loams are a mixture of clay, sand and silt, creating the best soils for growing a wide range of plants successfully. Where clays dominate the mixture they are described as heavy loams; otherwise they are sandy or light loams. They are less prone to compaction or rain capping than clay and under good management, provide a good soil water regime for plant life.

Marls Marls are composed of clay and chalk. Marl is a term loosely applied to a range of soils based on these materials.

Peaty soils Being derived from decaying plant material, peats have a fibrous structure and a high moisture-holding capacity. Most are acid and suffer from low plant nutrient levels, and so consequently support a comparatively limited range of plants. Where the groundwater of peat deposits is derived from a calcareous rock – for example, from chalk, as in the East Anglian fens – they are neutral or slightly alkaline and make good productive soils when drained. When allowed to become too dry, the peat is destroyed by oxidation causing land levels to fall.

Organic matter

Because of its value as plant food, the single most important ingredient of

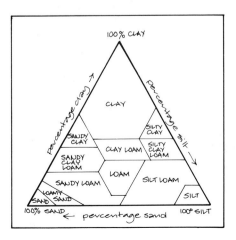

Figure 2.3 Analysis diagram for classification of soils.

topsoil is humus. In undisturbed soils, humus forms a dark brown or nearly black layer, found just under the surface layer of dead vegetation. It is created by soil organisms such as insects, protozoa, fungi and bacteria which decompose organic matter. Since they require oxygen they are absent in waterlogged or compacted soils where decomposition ceases and humus is no longer produced. So long as the humus layer is moist but the water level in the soil remains below it, soil organisms recycle all the organic debris into nutrients which are then absorbed by plant roots. Moreover, as humus absorbs and retains moisture, it helps plants to survive droughts. When planting on poor soils in particular, organic materials which decompose to form humus, should be introduced during their cultivation.

Soil water

The amount of water that can be held in the soil depends on a number of factors – for instance, depth, structure, texture, and organic matter content. These factors affect the amount of pore space present in the soil in which water can be stored. For example, a good agricultural loam can contain up to 50 per cent of volume of pore space. Compaction, on the other hand, as already stressed, reduces pore space substantially and can lead to problems of saturation, drainage and erosion.

Not all the water present in the soil is available to plants. Available water includes gravitational water – that is, water which is moving laterally or downwards under the influence of gravity once saturation (field capacity) has been exceeded. Available water also includes a proportion of the water held by capillary attraction in the fine and medium-sized soil pores. Some of this capillary action is held too tightly for plant roots to extract and is therefore 'unavailable'. The division between available and unavailable water is called the wilting point.

A final category of water is termed the hygroscopic water which is present as a thin film surrounding the finest soil particles. It is held so tightly that oven-drying is required to release it.

Soil air

Air in the soil is as necessary for plant growth as moisture, since plant roots

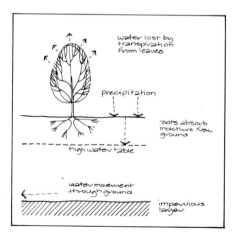

Figure 2.4   Movement of water after significant rainfall.

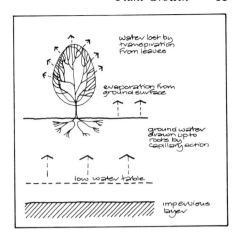

Figure 2.5   Water movement after dry weather.

must take up oxygen and expel carbon dioxide. The volume of air in the soil is governed by the spaces between the soil particles and the extent to which they are filled with water. Sandy soils have comparatively large air spaces, so can hold more air than clays. When a soil has become waterlogged or compacted, the air is expelled and if the anaerobic conditions continue, soil organisms and plant roots become asphyxiated and die.

Soil alkalinity or acidity (pH)

Another factor that determines the range of plants that will grow on a particular soil is its alkalinity or acidity. The degree of acidity or alkalinity is expressed as the 'pH', which is measured on a 14-point logarithmic scale: pH 7 is the neutral central point; below pH 7, soils are acid and above pH 7, they are alkaline. The pH of a soil is significant because it controls the availability of mineral nutrients to plants.

The widest range of ornamental plants can be grown in slightly acid soils between pH 5.7–6.7, which gives the optimum availability of nutrients. Above pH 7 the soils becomes more alkaline and plants such as ash, field maple and Wayfaring Tree thrive. Acid soils are favoured by pines, birches and heathers and have been colonized by invasive rhododendrons in the southern counties. A few plants, such as oak, holly and yew can tolerate a broad pH range, from pH 4–8. However, at extremes of soil acidity or alkalinity – that is, under 4 or over 9 – very few plants can survive.

It is possible to modify the pH of a soil, by the addition of 'ameliorants', but this can be expensive. It is more ecologically sound and more cost-effective to select plant material to suit the prevailing conditions. Plants establish more satisfactorily and management is simplified.

Plant nutrients

The soil is the source of the mineral nutrients necessary for plant growth which are taken up in solution through the roots. Nutrients dissolved in water can also be absorbed through the leaves, a method termed "foliar feeding".

Plants require three main elements in large quantities: nitrogen (N) for leaf and stem growth, phosphorus (P) for vigorous root development and potassium (K) to increase the production of flowers and seeds. These three are the major components of artificial inorganic fertilizers, sometimes supplemented by calcium, magnesium and sulphur which are needed in moderate amounts. Calcium may also be applied as lime or gypsum.

Minute quantities of several other elements are necessary for healthy plant development. These 'trace elements' are manganese, boron, zinc, iron, copper, chlorine, cobalt (for legumes only) and molybdenum. A deficiency, or excess in any of these elements causes growth abnormalities. Although the levels of nutrients in a soil may be adequate, they are sometimes unavailable to plants because of the soil acidity or alkalinity. The availability of the three major nutrients declines with both rising and falling pH. Where the soil pH is very high, iron cannot be absorbed, so causing a deficiency in the plants. This can be rectified by applying it as iron sequestrene. As the soil becomes more acid at lower pH levels, calcium becomes deficient, while iron, manganese and aluminium become available to toxic excess.

The availability of nutrients also depends on the soil structure. For example, an open-textured sandy soil is very free-draining, so nutrients applied to the surface are quickly leached away from the plant roots, unless organic materials are worked into the upper soil.

Organic manures, such as farmyard manure, spent mushroom compost, composted plant material such as leaf mould, or animal products such as hoof-and horn or dried blood, are decomposed by soil bacteria into a broad range of soluble nutrients which are then available to plants. Inorganic fertilizers are usually based on a calculated, balanced dose of the main nutrients, as a compound N-P-K fertilizer.

The main differences between organic and artificial fertilizers are:

1   The speed at which the nutrients are released into the soil. Artificial fertilizers dissolve quite rapidly, unless they are in slow-release granules. However, sulphate of potash is stable in the soil. Organic materials release the nutrients over a longer period of time.
2   Organic matter improves structure, whereas inorganic fertilizers do not.
3   The moisture-retaining capacity of a soil which has been enriched with a fibrous, organic manure or compost is enhanced. This helps plants to resist drought.
4   The nutrient balance of inorganic fertilizers can be specifically selected to suit a particular soil and its deficiencies, crop and season of the year. Most agricultural colleges carry out soil analyses, for a small fee, which includes a report on the shortages of nutrients and advice on remedial measures.

Plant Ecology

In many contexts, landscape design involves grouping together plants of diverse geographical origins, to achieve specific aesthetic or practical effects. Their survival, growth and the maintenance of the desired balance between them can only be ensured by continuing horticultural care.

In other situations, the landscape designer requires an understanding of natural plant communities; either when dealing with the conservation of native communities or when attempting partially to recreate semi-natural communities. It is important to recognize that the *de novo* creation of the full richness and balance of a long-established plant community (from flowering plants to mosses, fungi and the essential invertebrates and microbes) is never completely possible. 'Natural' planting therefore cannot be offered as an alternative to conservation of existing important habitats.

The natural distribution of plants is determined by the interaction of many environmental factors, which fall into five categories:

1 climatic factors, such as summer drought, frost sensitivity, and high summer humidity;
2 topographical factors, such as altitude, which closely interacts with the effects of climate;
3 soil-related or 'edaphic' factors – that is, soil type, including pH, drainage and salinity;
4 biotic factors – that is, the influence of all other living organisms, other plants, animals (especially grazing species), birds, insects, fungi, bacteria.

   Man is, strictly speaking, just another member of this list, but the effects of man's activities can be so much more complex, damaging and widespread than that of any other organism. For example, timber harvesting, agriculture, mineral extraction, extensive building projects and pollution are so damaging that man's influence is often considered separately.
5 Catastrophic events, such as fires, flooding and landslides.

Each plant species has an upper and lower tolerance limit for each environmental factor, which is, in turn, affected by interaction between them. Some factors only become critical at certain life stages – for instance, adequate sunlight may be needed to stimulate flowering or water for fruit formation. A plant's tolerance of all these environmental influences determines where it can thrive.

Apart from the influence of man, the most crucial direct biotic influence on plants is that of other plants. The immobility of each individual dictates that it is competing for finite resources of sunlight, water and minerals with all the plants around it. The strategies which plants have evolved in response to environmental conditions of stress or disturbance fall into three main categories:

1 'Competitors' have the ability to capture resources more successfully than other species, where conditions of growth are optimal and there is little stress or disturbance. They tend to be vigorous, tall-growing species, which make luxuriant vegetative growth during the summer and include nettles and rosebay willowherb.
2 'Stress tolerators' have evolved means of surviving one or more environmental extremes – such as infertility, extremes of pH, water shortage, shade or salinity – more successfully than most other plants. They tend to be compact and slow-growing, often continuing growth throughout the year, but are poor competitors. Examples are rock roses and thyme which can grow on shallow, alkaline soils.
3 'Ruderal' species are efficient colonizers of productive, disturbed ground, but are less able to compete in dense vegetation or to tolerate adverse environmental conditions. They tend to have a short life cycle and produce large quantities of seed, which have efficient distribution mechanisms. Man's activities, particularly agriculture and gardening, create ideal conditions for ruderals, such as groundsel, poppies and shepherd's purse.

Not many plants fall neatly into one of these categories. Many combinations of intermediate 'tactics' are possible that can enable plants to establish successfully in specific situations created by particular combinations of environmental factors.

This spectrum of adaptation to subtly different situations enables mixtures of species to thrive together. The plants in a woodland are able to share the resources of light, nutrients and water because all are stress tolerators or stress evaders. Distinct foliage layers are discernible; the dominant upper canopy trees (such as oak and ash), subsidiary trees (cherry, wild service tree), shrubs (holly, hawthorn), herbs (wood anemone, dog's mercury) and ground flora (mosses and liverworts). Stress evaders, such as primroses and bluebells, flower before the trees come into leaf, whilst there is light at ground level.

A plant 'community' is defined as an assemblage of plants occurring together in a specific place, which is sufficiently characteristic as a group to be named and recognized in other places. Whilst there is a universally accepted framework for naming individual plants, this is not the case for the description and naming of plant communities. A variety of analytical methods are in use, based on data from sample areas (or quadrats), but the simplest method, which is usually most appropriate in the landscape context, is the description and identification of a community by the species or type of plant which predominates by virtue of being the largest or most abundant – for example, an oak wood or a heather heath. A community may be described by habitat factors – for example, a chalk grassland or a maritime heath. In fact, the identification of particular plant communities can be a more reliable indicator of prevailing environmental conditions than direct measurements of physical factors. For instance, patches of bracken can indicate the drier, least exposed areas on a hillside.

It is of fundamental importance to realize that plant communities are not static systems. Their species composition changes, in some cases very slowly, and the dynamics are far from fully understood. There seem to be different patterns of change, cycle and succession.

When bare land is colonized by plants, a sequence of vegetational changes is observed. Species establish, increase in numbers when environmental factors are optimal for them and then dwindle as the environment changes so a succession of plant communities occurs. The particular species that arrive and the order in which they appear depends on chance, the availability of seed, topography and season, so characteristic successions can only be described in general terms.

It was once thought that, if uninterrupted by man or natural catastrophe, every succession would eventually culminate in a 'climatic climax' community that would remain stable in its species composition until a change in the climate occurred, such as the coming and going of Ice Ages. However, we have been studying plant communities for a very short period of time. It may be that,

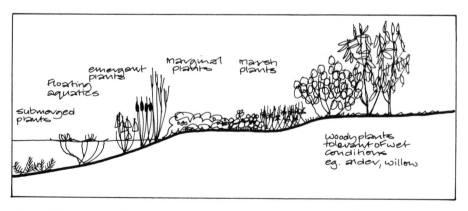

Figure 2.6 A waterside plant community exhibits a range of adaptions to differing degrees of immersion.

whilst changes occur fairly rapidly in the early stages, the later, more stable communities also change, over longer spans of time than we have adequate records for, or incorporate local changes on shorter cycles.

When a succession is beginning in a nutrient-poor situation, such as on disturbed soil or a demolition site, plant nutrients and water may be very scarce, and so the first species able to establish are particularly stress-tolerant. They will probably be a mixture of tree, shrub and herb seedlings but the growth of the trees and shrubs may be stunted in the early stages. Eventually they may develop a canopy that creates too much shade for the early herb colonizers to survive and their place may be taken by shade-tolerant herbaceous species.

Where existing soil, which is already capable of supporting vegetation, has been laid bare by fire or cultivation, the soil is already rich in plant nutrients. In this case, of the many seeds arriving on the scene, the first to germinate are usually the ruderal species, whose short life span may enable them to succeed in setting seed before the tall, dense growth of better competitors, like rosebay willowherb and thistles, overwhelm them. Most tree seedlings stand a poor chance of establishing amongst such aggressive competitors. It may be several years before some local physical disturbance creates a space where a tree sapling can develop. Once it grows above the height of the competitive herbs, its spreading canopy begins to cast more shade than they can tolerate. Their numbers then dwindle and the limited range of herb species characteristic of the woodland floor which have efficient dispersal systems, like ivy, may be able to move in.

Some of the long-unchanged plant communities that we value are an intermediate stage in a succession that has been held in a static state by artificial means – for example, grazing or fire. An example is chalk grassland, which is maintained as a rich mixture of short grasses and colourful herbaceous species by sheep- or rabbit-grazing. If the sheep are removed, the dead leaves of the taller-growing grasses create a dense litter and these plants soon outcompete the grassland herbs. Seedlings of hawthorn can flourish and, within a few years, an impenetrable scrub will develop.

This demonstrates the importance of management in the conservation of a plant community in the particular state that we value. Other examples are the cyclical coppicing of woodland and the burning or light grazing of heather moorlands.

Soil fertility plays a crucial role in determining the balance between stress-tolerant and competitor species in a plant community. Again, an agriculturally unimproved herb-rich grassland which has long been maintained by grazing or hay harvesting is a good example. The annual removal of vegetation prevents the build-up of blanketing litter and the many herbaceous flowers can tolerate the low nutrient levels better than the competitive grasses. The application of a fertilizer to this community could enable the potentially more vigorous grasses present to grow so much more luxuriantly that they would quickly predominate, ousting the flowering herbs.

This introduction to the influences on, and interactions within, natural plant communities can only begin to indicate their complexity. The creation of herb-rich grasslands or of woodland with some attributes of our old, deciduous woods, is potentially the source of great visual delight. However, such schemes can fail due to the designer's lack of understanding of plants' reactions to environmental factors or appreciation of plants' strategies. The advice of an ecologist is essential to the success of naturalistic planting projects.

CHAPTER 3

Site Survey and Analysis

Site Survey

When assessing the potential of a site, whether for development or for improvement, it is necessary to undertake a site survey at the outset. The survey should include the following factual information about the site:

- Location and type of site boundaries
- Local climate
- Topography
- Geology and soils
- Water and drainage
- Access and circulation
- Land-use, and that of adjoining land
- Existing vegetation
- Wildlife
- Existing buildings, structures and historical features
- Services
- Views from within and without

At the survey stage, it is important to gain information about the planning background as far as the land in question is concerned. This would include its status in relation to the Local Plan conservation areas, listed buildings, tree preservation orders, ancient monuments, sites of special scientific interest, areas of outstanding natural beauty, areas liable to flooding, easements and rights of way. Of the above, those aspects most relevant to planting design are examined below:

Location and site boundaries

Detailed information on the location of the site, adjacent buildings, rights of way, overhead services, main archaeological features, contours and bench mark levels can be obtained from Ordnance Survey maps.

Site boundaries should be checked to avoid possible future disputes over maintenance of walls, fences, trees and hedges. If the legal position is unclear, it is important to resolve uncertainty about ownership and future management of the boundaries before any changes are made to them.

Local climate

Information about the climate of the area as a whole may be obtained from the local weather centre. Knowledge of average and exceptional rainfalls is important for drainage design. Information on the prevailing wind directions at different times of the year should be established and the site should be examined to assess the microclimate. This would include identifying the areas exposed to the strongest winds and the sheltered areas; the sunny and more shaded areas; and potential frost pockets.

Topography

An accurate contour plan is essential for most large sites. On smaller sites and where level changes are not great, a grid of spot-levels or information about specific levels may be more appropriate.

Geology and soils

Geological information about the locality in general can be obtained from the solid and drift maps published by the Ordnance Survey for the Geological Survey of Great Britain. More detailed information about the site itself can be found from a soil survey using an appropriate number of samples or from trial pits. The information on soils should include the soil types, their acidity or alkalinity (pH), fertility, texture, degree of compaction and depths of topsoil and subsoil. These factors often vary widely, even within one parcel of land. Subsoil drainage tests are commonly carried out at the same time.

Water and drainage

Areas of surface water, liability to flooding, springs, ditches and ponds should all be recorded. Field drainage systems or other subsoil drains and outfalls should be traced as far as possible and records of any existing surface water drains obtained (see also p.20 'Services').

Existing vegetation and ecology

A detailed vegetation survey is important because the retention of existing, healthy trees and other significant vegetation greatly benefits any development from the outset, enhancing both its character and amenity value.

This survey should show the positions of woodlands, groups of trees and individual trees, together with hedges and expanses of scrub vegetation. Important ground-cover vegetation should also be plotted and identified. BS 5837 : 1980 'Trees in relation to construction' emphasizes the importance of carrying out a tree survey at the pre-planning stage. The position of trees with a stem diameter of 75mm and above, at a height of 1.4m above ground level, should be accurately plotted and their characteristics should then be described on a related schedule. This should include the tree tag number, the species, approximate height and spread, the girth, the height of the lowest main branch, the amenity value and condition. The amenity value should be assessed by the landscape architect as part of this survey. Because of his training and experience he can assess the relative visual importance of the vegetation in a balanced manner. It is also necessary to evaluate the physical condition of the trees in order to establish priorities for retention and the advice of an arboriculturalist should be sought.

The amenity value of each tree may be graded as follows:

AA   essential   – to be retained at all costs
A   important   – to be retained
B   desirable   – to be kept unless retention makes the project unworkable
C   non-essential – to be kept or not as planning or overall planting require
D   undesirable – to be removed because diseased, dangerous, dead or
                   overcrowded

The physical condition of each tree may be classified in the schedule in a similar manner:

VG   – very good
G   – good
F   – fair
P   – poor
S   – suppressed

These two scales need to be considered together in the assessment of individual trees, or groups of trees, for retention. For example, a tree which is rated highly in visual terms (A or AA) but in fair physical condition (F) may be selected for

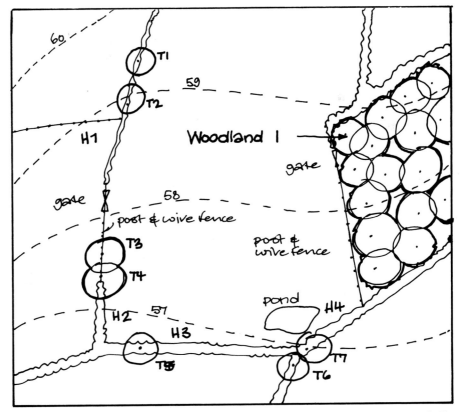

Figure 3.1 A sketch site survey plan which records existing features including vegetation, landform and boundaries.

retention and improved by tree surgery.

Ancient trees that are part of an historic scene will eventually have to be replaced by new planting. There are many examples of this, like the ancient limes that form an avenue to the Old Royal Greenwich Observatory. Wherever possible, new trees should be planted some years in advance of the felling of old trees, so that when they are lost there is continuity. To maintain continuity of an avenue, the new trees should be planted parallel to the existing line, but not so near that they are likely to be damaged when the overmature trees are felled.

Where there are trees of great age, of special significance or apparently in a dangerous condition, a professionally qualified aboriculturalist should be called in to make a specialist assessment on their health and recommend immediate and future treatment. This is especially important where public liability may be involved. An example would be where trees overhang a public footpath.

Wildlife

Evidence, principally of rabbits and deer, should be noted and measures may need to be taken to protect new plants, either individually, or in groups.

Existing buildings, structures and historical features

Existing buildings should be precisely surveyed. They may create sheltered spaces or, if tall, shade large areas to the north, increase wind speed and create turbulence, especially if there are wind funnels between blocks. The levels of damp-proof courses, basement windows, steps, pavings and drains around buildings should be recorded.

Services

The routes of all existing above- and below-ground services and ancillary structures should be plotted on the survey. Data may be available from the utility company concerned. This information may not be precise, so trial excavations are sometimes necessary to determine exact locations of underground services. The utility company can provide information on the restrictions which they need to impose on development, earthworks or planting in the vicinity of their services in order to maintain a safe supply.

Site Analysis

The purpose of the analysis is to determine those factors derived from evaluation of the site survey information, which are likely to influence the planning and layout.

Experience in assessing many different types of land and vegetation is an essential part of the landscape architect's contribution. The site analysis drawing would show, for example, the main visual enclosure and open spaces formed by the existing vegetation and by the underlying landforms. The extent and quality of the views out of and into the site would suggest the need for new planting and/or groundshaping to enhance the most attractive views or to screen off unattractive features. Visually important ridgelines, steep slopes identified by slope analysis, or areas liable to flooding would suggest areas where it would generally be inappropriate or difficult to site buildings.

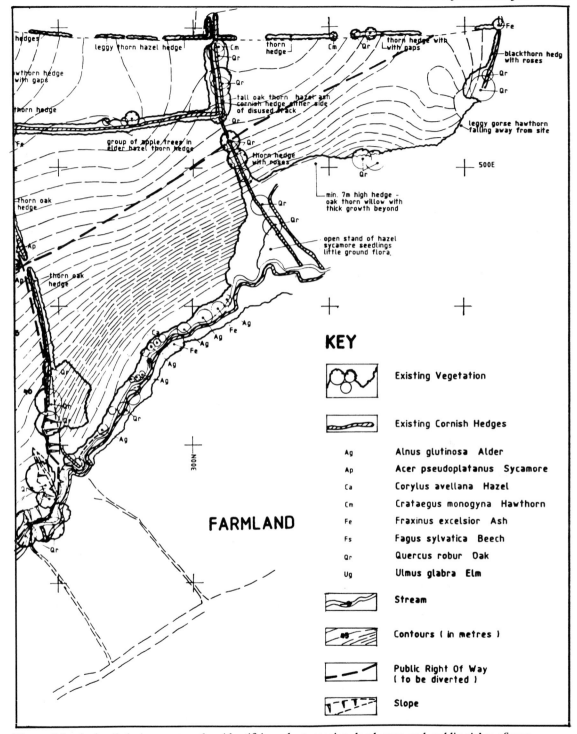

KEY

⬭	Existing Vegetation
▱	Existing Cornish Hedges
Ag	Alnus glutinosa Alder
Ap	Acer pseudoplatanus Sycamore
Ca	Corylus avellana Hazel
Cm	Crataegus monogyna Hawthorn
Fe	Fraxinus excelsior Ash
Fs	Fagus sylvatica Beech
Qr	Quercus robur Oak
Ug	Ulmus glabra Elm
~	Stream
~	Contours (in metres)
– –	Public Right Of Way (to be diverted)
⊤⊤⊤	Slope

Figure 3.2 A detailed site survey plan identifying plant species, land uses and public rights of way.

CHAPTER 4

The Design Process

The dynamics of landscape introduce the need to consider the fourth dimension, that of time, into the design process. Many other art forms are limited in their concept to two or three dimensions. Sculpture and buildings, for example, do not, of themselves, undergo great change other than those induced by weathering. The effect of time on the development and maturity of a landscape needs to be considered in terms of both the structural and sculptural changes of the landscape and the way in which these changes are managed to achieve the design concept. The design concept is therefore only a part of the design process. The methods to be used to implement the concept, and the decisions on how the scheme is to be maintained and managed, are all essential elements of the process of landscape design.

The initial part of this process from inception to sketch design is concerned principally with exploring and developing the client's brief in relation to the opportunities and constraints offered by the project and the site. Ideally, where multi-professional design teams are involved in projects, this is the time when the site development strategy should be evolved. The juxtaposition of all the main elements of the project should be considered and determined. It is particularly important that the landscape architect should be involved in this process and assist with the siting of buildings and the arrangement of the landscape spaces that arise between them. The siting of roads and footpaths should have a close relationship to landform, existing vegetation structures and existing buildings. Today, underground services are often grouped into service 'corridors' to make access easier and to allow for freedom in designing the main 'structure' of the planting. The results of this part of the design process should be a site development or landscape strategy plan, combining the architectural, engineering and landscape design elements – the Strategic Development Plan.

Normally, the plan in draft form is related to an outline cost plan. Design budget costs may need adjustment before the plan is finally accepted by the client. In some instances, the Strategic Development Plan may form the basis of the planning application. Much depends on the nature of the scheme and the requirements of the planning authority.

The next stage is to work the scheme up into greater detail. Design drawings are produced to identify the position, species, size, number or density of all the proposed trees, shrubs and ground-cover plants. At the same time, other related aspects of soft landscaping are considered, such as minor groundshaping, soil cultivation, the incorporation of ameliorants and the type and depth of mulch to be used. This information should be annotated on the detail design drawings, which may be required to supplement the application to the local planning authority for permission to develop land.

More importantly perhaps, it is the detail of these drawings that is used to check cost against the cost plan. They assist the quantity surveyor, where one is employed, to prepare Bills or Schedules of Quantity.

However, the main purpose of the detail design drawings is to convey sufficient information for a contractor to prepare prices and to carry out a scheme. With the Specification and the Bills or Schedules of Quantity, the detail design drawings form a package which should allow a contractor to price the work more accurately. Moreover, where several contractors are invited to price the work on a competitive basis, this 'tender package' allows contractors to price the work on the same basis.

The extent and complexity of planting influences the amount of detail required on the planting plans. For example, for estimating or for work on-site, a woodland could be planted from a small-scale general arrangement plan, together with a representative area drawn to larger scale. On the other hand, a planting plan for a complex shrub or herbaceous border should show the position and quantity of each species.

In practice, planting plans are drawn to a wide range of scales, to suit different purposes:

- 1:1000 to 1:5000 are used for concept plans or Strategic Development Plans.
- 1:500 general arrangement drawings are used for large industrial projects or major shelter planting schemes covering several hectares.
- 1:100 or 1:200 drawings are used for tree and shrub planting schemes where each species is to be planted in sizable groups – for example, within a park or for a housing development.
- 1:50 drawings are used for detailed or small-scale planting schemes, such as small planting areas amongst a group of buildings.
- 1:10 or 1:20 drawings are used for very detailed areas of planting, such as small courtyard designs.

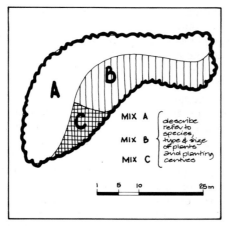

Figure 4.1   A general arrangement planting plan, suitable for large projects, to be used in conjunction with a schedule.

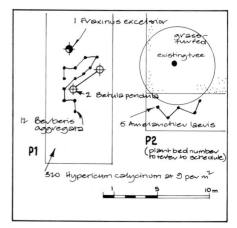

Figure 4.2   A planting plan suitable for general arrangement of shrubs and trees using the British Standard symbols for different tree sizes. (BS 1192 : Part 4).

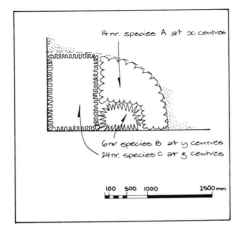

Figure 4.3 *Above:* Detailed planting plan for small planting areas near buildings, to be used with schedule.

Figure 4.4 *Right:* The planting shown on this plan, as envisaged by the designer.

As the overall concept is developed, areas of a scheme are worked up at a larger scale, to show greater detail.

Generally, the planting plans should show the full extent of planting beds in relation to their surroundings – existing trees, terraces, steps, external doors and pathways. Plants may either be named in full on the plan or be given reference letters that refer to a key on the plan. The number of plants in each group of the same species should also be shown. The spacing may be included on the planting plan or given in the schedule of plant material on the drawing. This schedule of plant material should include the standardized international (Latin) name of each plant, the total number of plants, their size, quality and planting density.

Following implementation and practical completion, a period of measured maintenance is carried out. For many landscape contracts, a period of 12 months' maintenance is included to run concurrently with a 12-month defects liability period. This has the advantage of the same contractor being responsible for the establishment of the plants. In some instances, it may be appropriate to extend this period to 18 or even 24 months.

Because a landscape design always takes a number of years to become established and to reach the approximate form envisaged in the original design, it is important to discuss with the client, in the initial briefing, what arrangements are to be made for the future management and maintenance of the site. Maintenance schedules may be required to identify specific operations that should be carried out at regular intervals. This work may be implemented by the client's own workforce or contractors separately appointed for this purpose. With all, but particularly on larger schemes a Management Plan should be produced, dealing with the short- and long-term strategy of how the new landscape is to be maintained and managed. It may extend further than dealing solely with plant maintenance and give advice about the size and type of workforce that will need to be employed and the type and number of specific kinds of machinery that will be necessary to carry out the work over the seasons.

CHAPTER 5

Design with Planting

Unity and Simplicity

> 'Unity is a quality found in all great landscape.' (Sylvia Crowe, *Garden Design* p.76)

Unity may be achieved in a number of different ways. For example, the use of a certain range of species, materials or artefacts running through a composition, like key musical themes, can provide a unifying element. A strong focal point which dominates other elements in the design or the repetition of design motifs or details can also help to achieve unity.

The use of a single plant species throughout a scheme as the dominant element, with other materials complementing or contrasting with it, can be most effective for the smaller-scale design. Limiting the variety of plants and colour range has a strong unifying effect. On a larger scale, the natural colours and topography of the local landscape can be echoed in the design to form a sound basis for design unity within and beyond the boundaries of the site.

Lest the discipline of unity be too slavishly applied, Brenda Colvin in *Land and Landscape*, sounded a note of warning: 'unity, if it imposes monotonous repetition and conformity, is sterile' (p.134).

The strength of a scheme in both large scale and detailed design may derive from the application of the principle of simplicity. Too much ornamentation can undermine the strength of a design, by creating a restless and spotty appearance. For instance, a mixture of strikingly coloured flowering shrubs will compete with each other to their general detriment. A random mixture of plants lacks positive impact because it is without a clear structure or overall theme.

Simplicity can be especially important in the large scale, where broad masses of tree planting are often used to define major spaces. Where this planting forms a backdrop to buildings, or more intricate shrubs or herbaceous planting, simplicity of form and colour are essential.

Scale and Proportion

'Scale and proportion are themselves attributes of unity, for without them, there can be no harmony of design' (Sylvia Crowe, *Garden Design* p.82) Consideration of these factors, and their relationship to each other, is an important part of the design process.

As a guide, objects generally appear smaller outdoors, so that a more spacious treatment is desirable. For example, paths should be wider to avoid looking narrow and pinched, steps should be shallower with broader treads to avoid appearing steep and potentially dangerous.

Normal eye level is the critical height for visual perception. This determines the way in which people experience and enjoy most spatial design. Different effects are achieved in planting design, depending on whether the planting is above or below eye level. Where the main users are likely to be children, it is their eye level which should determine the critical height. The spatial requirements for adults' sheltered sitting spaces, teenagers' informal kickabouts and toddlers' play spaces all differ. The means of enclosure should be in proportion and appropriate to the users and the function. Small areas take on a different character when enclosed by a tall hedge, or a wall, as opposed to low shrubs. Larger areas can be successfully enclosed with substantial masses of trees.

Speed of Movement

Small-scale, intricate planting patterns are appropriate where people pass close to them, walk slowly or sit amongst them, as in an enclosed garden. When travelling fast through a landscape, it appears as a meaningless blur if the scale is not adjusted to compensate for the speed of movement. Therefore, alongside a road, mainly for through traffic, both planting masses and the intervening spaces should be generous in scale. Avenues, or lines of trees planted along roadsides or railways over long distances can be distracting and irritating at speed. Where there is also a footpath, a pedestrian scale of planting can be used to indicate slower speeds and the need for of extra care.

Perspective in Design

Perspective plays a most important part in landscape design, since few features are ever seen in true elevation. Hills appear to have much steeper gradients in prospect than they have in reality. When looking downhill, apparent distance and slope increases, sometimes quite dramatically. Distant objects appear even further from hilltops than they are in reality. These are all stimulating to the observer used to flat landscapes.

The apparent distance and depth in a design can be increased in a number of ways. Masses of fine-textured plants, particularly those with blue flowers or grey leaves, appear to recede and so can enhance the sense of distance if planted in the background. Conversely, hot, strong colours in the foreground against foliage in the background has the opposite effect. A smooth-textured surface, such as close-mown grass, gives an impression of space.

Distance can be gained by concealing a boundary in shadow, or by making it recede into the surrounding landscape by planting on either side, so that the eye is carried beyond, by the continuity of foliage. An uninterrupted straight boundary seems longer than one which is articulated or punctuated – for instance by broad spreading trees.

Many devices have been used in the past to increase the apparent size of gardens and landscapes. The 'ha-ha' was introduced in the eighteenth century as a concealed barrier to prevent stock from the surrounding estate gaining access to lawns or ornamental areas close to the manor house. Selected views from the house were therefore achieved without obstruction by fences or hedges.

Groundshaping can be used positively to improve the sense of scale and to give contrast in flat surroundings, although it can be costly unless surplus soil is

Figure 5.1 Planting at different heights to aid spatial definition and visual control.

Figure 5.2 Simple plant layers which are useful for analysis and design.

Figure 5.3 Small scale variety is appropriate where people can appreciate planting whilst walking past.

Figure 5.4   Hedges of differing heights define spaces of differing qualities.

available. Glastonbury Tor is more effective, rising above the Somerset Levels, than it could ever be in the Lake District.

Perspective can be falsified, from one direction only, by, for example, planting hedges on either side of a space to a taper or by tapering a long pond, to artificially enhance the sense of distance. The ultimate in such artificiality is the use of a painted or constructed *trompe d'oeil* to suggest a non-existent view. For example, the scene at Kenwood is completed by a white-painted timber 'elevation' of a classic bridge.

Focal Points and Views

The main focus of a design may be an important building, a water feature, sculpture, or a distant view. Certain landscape design principles can be used to lead the eye to a focal point:

1   An object in full sun stands out when contrasted with a shady area as does a light-coloured object seen against a dark background.
2   Paths can be arranged to guide people to a focal point. Movement draws the eye, especially when human activity is involved, so others will tend to follow.
3   Attention can be drawn to a particular feature by framing the view.

Openings below tree canopies can provide excellent visual frames for views of buildings, a local feature or distant scenery. A more formal frame can be created by trimmed hedges or trees to create a precise, geometric opening. On a smaller scale, windows can be formed in a yew hedge, such is its tolerance of topiary.

4 An avenue of trees or corridor of shrubs can be used to focus the eye on an object of interest.

5 Points of specific interest or focus can actually be located *within* the mass of framework planting, like alcoves or window seats in the thickness of the building wall.

Mass planting can be used as a background to buildings, sculptures, or to groups of plants which have been designed to provide points of colour and detailed interest. The background planting should be simple and restrained rather than assertive, avoiding plants with strong leaf texture or flower, fruit or foliage characteristics, which might divert the eye from foreground interest.

Plants themselves can also be trained to form architectural features. Large shrubs or trees such as lime or beech, can be planted and trained so that the foliage eventually interlocks and forms a 'bower' for shade, shelter and privacy, or a tunnel over a pathway.

Structure Planting

Planting which defines the larger spaces and creates the broad forms within a site is widely referred to as structure planting. It can be used to define the areas

Figure 5.5 Perspective is falsified here at Herrenhausen, by hedges planted on converging lines.

Figure 5.6   Enclosing hedges creating off-set vistas. A focal point leads the eye to the next change of direction.

Figure 5.7   Gently curving paths enclosed by hedges raise interest and encourage exploration.

Figure 5.8   Mass structure planting, such as these solid walls of trees can create impressive outdoor spaces.

Figure 5.9 A substantial framework of trees divides space without creating a total screen.

required for different functions within a site, to give emphasis to the landform, help to integrate a site with its surroundings or provide vistas of distant objects outside the site. Because of their stature and longevity trees form the basis of structure planting. A management plan for areas of structure planting is essential, to ensure that the faster-growing trees are removed at an early stage and planned maintenance, including thinning, is carried out at appropriate intervals.

This type of planting does not necessarily have to be massive in scale, like the solid 'walls' of trees at Versailles. A suggestion of spatial definition can be given by strategically placed trees as in the English landscape tradition where freestanding groups of trees create much less rigid spaces associated with a more informal semi-natural landscape. On a smaller scale, outdoor 'rooms' can be created by clipped hedges, such as those at Sissinghurst or Hidcote.

A hard physical barrier is frequently unnecessary. A line of trees can effectively indicate spatial division, although below their canopies only the trunks or side branches interrupt the view. Conversely, hedgerow trees – such as field maple, ash, holly and oak – planted at intervals in hedges, give them greater significance as a dividing structure in the countryside.

Effective screen and shelter planting usually requires both trees and shrubs. The proportion of evergreen to deciduous plants may depend on whether visual screening is to be a significant requirement, whether year-round shelter is desirable, whether a seasonal emphasis is required, or whether evergreens are to be located so as to allow winter sun to penetrate.

Careful analysis of the species and structure of local woodlands and hedgerows can help the designer to achieve similar composition in new shelter planting, and so help to relate new developments in rural settings to the existing landscape.

Surface Modelling

A valuable device for sites with limited topographical variation or interest is the use of shrubs or trees to accentuate even quite small differences in surface levels. For instance, an impression of height can be increased by planting dense, tall-growing shrubs on the crest of a low rise in the ground, with short-mown grass in the hollows. The effect can be developed further if the shrubs themselves can be contoured by careful selection of species, with low, finer-

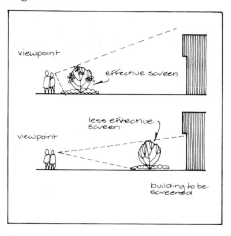

Figure 5.10   Relationship between positioning and effectiveness of low screen planting.

leaved plants like *Lonicera pileata* or *Cotoneaster conspicuus 'Decorus'* nearest the viewer, medium-leaved species like dogwood in the centre ground and larger-leaved, taller-growing shrubs like laurels on the summit of the ridge.

Screening and Privacy

Screen planting is intended to restrict the view of a particular object, building or scene to some extent. It may also provide shelter, privacy and enclosure. Screening should be sited as near as is practicable to the viewpoint or to nearby routes from which views can be obtained. If this can be achieved, a relatively small amount of carefully positioned screen planting can be sufficient.

When selecting plants for a screen, consideration should be given to the desired density of the screen and the growth rates of the plants selected, as well as their appropriateness for the situation. The speed of movement past the object or building that is to be screened may also affect the design of the screen and its appearance to the viewer. For example, should the screen form a feature in its own right, incorporating interest through intricacy of detail or should it be dense, unobtrusive and evergreen?

The composition of large-scale screening, which is designed to help integrate difficult and often conflicting developments with an area of largely natural landscape, should be based on the use of native plant material.

It may not be possible, or for that matter desirable, to screen the whole of larger-scale building complexes. However, the main visual problem, and the element typical of large industrial developments that largely gives an indication of scale, is the inevitable low-level clutter of parked vehicles, small ancillary buildings, stored materials, security fences and so on. If this low-level clutter can be screened with bold tree and shrub planting then the ability to integrate large structures successfully as simple geometric shapes into the landscape is more easily achieved. If space is available, screen planting can be reinforced by placing it on earth mounds. Shrubs with foliage reaching to the ground can also effectively screen comparatively small but unsightly structures, such as electrical substations.

Fast-growing, but relatively short-lived trees, like birch, alder, willow and poplar, can provide rapid initial screening, before slower-growing, longer-lived species like oaks and beech become effective and provide the long-term screening. Evergreens should also be included. To form a complete screen to ground level, trees can be supplemented with an understorey of shrubs, or hedges may be planted alongside. Where possible it is an advantage to establish screen planting in advance of sites being developed. Some hedges, such as beech or hornbeam, have a special value as they retain their dead leaves through the winter.

Trees

Trees chosen for a particular situation must be appropriate to the space, taking into consideration their potential ultimate size. This is particularly important where trees are to be planted near buildings or roads.

Given sufficient space, our native forest trees are entirely in scale with larger buildings. A single, carefully selected large-growing tree in a strategic position can provide an important point of interest and help to soften the possibly harsh outline of a building. Small trees can appear insignificant in relation to buildings many times their size or larger outdoor spaces. In fact it may lead to a weak design if trees are chosen principally for their flowers or autumn colour, rather than for their overall form and mass. Tall-growing trees grouped within, and adjacent to, extensive groups of buildings (like leisure centres or industrial complexes) can visually unify the skyline. To ensure the continuity of trees that are in key positions in a design composition, space must be provided alongside for their eventual replacement.

On a smaller scale, a single, suitable tree can emphasize the importance of a space, by becoming the focal point in, for example, a courtyard within a building or group of buildings. Trees have special value in courtyards or squares, by

Figure 5.11   A screen of shrub planting is an attractive means of providing domestic privacy.

Figure 5.12   Fast growing trees can effectively break up the mass of large modern buildings.

providing shade and helping to reduce glare or reflection. They can also increase privacy by reducing visibility through the canopy. They should, however, be selected to allow sufficient sunlight into restricted spaces, particularly in northern districts. Here trees with lighter foliage, such as ash, birch or false acacia may be the best choice.

Groups of trees, or a more formal row, can make a valuable contribution to the relationship between a landscape and a building, or a complex of buildings. Conversely, a number of trees dispersed in a random manner do not create a positive tie between the two.

A compact group of trees of the same species, planted close together, can take on the appearance of a single multi-stemmed specimen as they grow and mature, mimicking a natural occurrence. Not only do they have a greater visual effect than a solitary large tree, but continuity can be ensured should two or three die early.

Growth rates of trees vary considerably, according to the species and environmental conditions. The life span of alder and birch is comparatively short, but trees such as oak and beech can live for several centuries.

Woodlands

At the other end of the scale, tree-planting for shelter, screening or large-scale strategic planting utilizes more extensive copses or woodlands. There are four main questions to address when designing massed tree-planting.

1 What size of plantation would be visually satisfying in relation to the scale of the open spaces or enclosures of the surrounding landscape?
2 What shape of woodland outline would be sympathetic to the underlying landform and how can the shape be related to existing topographical features?
3 How should the pattern of species, the margins and the internal spaces be designed to create a sufficient sense of diversity and visual interest?
4 In considering the opportunities for conservation and recreation, are these aspects particularly affected by the detailed design and proposed system of woodland management?

Shrubs and Hedges

Shrubs vary in size from low, ground-hugging plants like the dwarf heathers, to species like rhododendrons and laurels which can grow to some six metres high or more. There is a wide range of species to suit almost every site, climate, soil condition, and a wide range of functions.

Shrubs mature faster than trees, some in as little as two to five years and generally have a shorter life span. For instance, the brooms have to be replaced every five to seven years. Some shrubs can only be maintained in vigorous

Figure 5.13 A single tree can be the focal point within a group of buildings.

Figure 5.14   Seating backed by shrub planting above eye-level because it offers a sense of security and privacy, as well as shelter.

health by pruning to encourage new growth. The range of species within each major genus, like the roses, camellias, heaths and rhododendrons, is extremely wide and the characteristics of individual species and their rates of growth differ considerably. The fact is underlined by the many specialist books devoted to each of these plant families.

As a design element, shrubs are used to provide the middle layer between the upper tree layer and the lower herbaceous layers. In this intermediate layer their principal role is one of space division and enclosure. The ultimate height of the shrub planting can be used to achieve a number of visual effects. For example, planting at knee height can create positive spatial definition without impeding views. Waist high planting can define routes, provide property boundaries or form protective barriers. Eye-level planting, forming a more substantial barrier, emphasizes visual enclosure and begins to frame views with openings, or screen them. Shrub planting above eye level provides privacy as well as enclosure. However, if privacy is required immediately, then a fence or wall should form the initial part of the screen.

In the same way that trees can become a nuisance through root or canopy spread, vigorous shrubs can quickly outgrow a particular space. In confined spaces, or alongside paths, it is important to select shrubs, other than clipped hedges, which, when mature, do not require regular pruning to limit their height or outward spread.

Traditionally, the main function of hedges was to define ownership boundaries, provide shelter and to confine stock. In addition to these roles, hedges provide a more formal means of space division or barrier within a design. As with general shrub planting, the visual effect of a hedge will depend upon the height at which it is maintained.

Climbers and Wall Shrubs

These are a valuable group of plants to the designer. They take up less space than hedges and can be used on a trellis to screen or to enclose. They are essential for clothing pergolas. Where space permits, they can also be used to relieve the monotony of extensive walls or fences either on their own, or with other planting. Climbers requiring support are easier to control than vigorous self-clinging varieties.

Ground-cover Plants

The lowest-growing layer of a planting design is usually low ground-hugging plants like Pachysandra or prostrate juniper, or by a grass or grass/herb ground cover (p.81). These low-growing plants are used to provide a carpet of vegetation providing complete cover as a single element, or in conjunction with trees and shrubs or other plant material. Ground-cover planting can be used to provide visual continuity in a design. Once established, its maintenance is generally more economic than grass, which may be an important design consideration.

Ground-cover plants can be selected from a variety of forms ranging from carpet-forming prostrate plants to low hummock-formers. Where ground-cover planting is used in conjunction with deciduous trees and shrubs evergreen species are particularly useful.

Herbaceous Plants and Bulbs

The use of herbaceous planting in relation to general landscape work needs to

Figure 5.15   Climbers can be used to relieve the monotony of extensive walls.

Figure 5.16   Climbers on a supporting frame offer a quick means of creating enclosure.

be carefully considered. Some useful evergreen perennials are in common usage and are appropriate for incorporation into design schemes where they will not suffer from the possibility of trampling. However, their generally soft and more fragile nature usually restricts their use to garden and small-scale schemes. Exceptionally, drifts of herbaceous plants, such as bluebells in woodlands where there is little trampling of the woodland floor, can be extremely effective. One of the main advantages of herbaceous planting is the interest that can be created within a scheme by strong points of colour in key positions, especially in the spring and autumn.

Grasses

Grass is used extensively as a simple ground-cover material. It is generally relatively cheap to create grass areas, but they can be extremely expensive to maintain as a closely-mown sward. In amenity landscape it provides the basic surface for spaces devoted to casual and active recreation. When allowed to grow long in conjunction with wild flowers it can be economically maintained as a relatively wild area that attracts butterflies, bees and small mammals.

The selection of appropriate grass mixes for use, soil type and climate is important and care should always be taken with soil preparation and initial establishment. Different planting techniques, from sowing to turfing and hydraulic-seeding, are possible but need to be considered in relation to the site and the brief.

Ornamental grasses can create points of interest in a design and act as a contrast to adjoining large-leaved ground cover or shrubs.

Figure 5.17   Ornamental grasses can create points of interest in a design.

CHAPTER 6

Plants: The Functional Role

In addition to their important visual role in the landscape, massed trees and shrubs can fulfil other specific practical functions.

Traditionally, trees were planted *en masse* in certain locations to form shelter belts, to improve the micro-climate. In urban areas, they can be used to filter dust from polluted air and on slopes their root structure assists in soil stabilization. Planting alone is generally not effective in achieving significant noise reduction, but psychologically it can play a beneficial role in reducing the effects of noise.

Wind Shelter

Vegetation can reduce wind speed locally over buildings or crops, because it is flexible and semi-permeable. The careful location of hedges or shelter belts can help to maximize the use of an exposed site at a moderate cost. The extent of shelter provided is governed by the height and density of the belt.

A solid barrier, such as a wall or closeboarded fence provides good shelter on the lee side over a distance up to two or three times its height, but eddies do occur on the lee side in strong winds. The practical use of solid or near-solid barriers for shelter is limited to small outdoor spaces associated with buildings, such as walled gardens.

A semi-permeable barrier can be more effective in that it can reduce wind speeds on its lee side for a distance of up to twenty to thirty times its height. A combination of trees and shrubs is ideal. The trees form the upper layer, whilst the shrubs extend the shelter from the tree canopy to ground level.

It is an advantage to mix evergreen and deciduous species. The proportion of evergreens should be at least 50 per cent, and preferably 65 per cent, to maintain effective shelter in winter. An important characteristic of shelter planting is that it grows to adopt a profile which is shaped by the wind.

Air Quality

Plants *en masse* have several appreciable effects on air quality.

1   They take up groundwater and release it back into the atmosphere, cooling the air and increasing humidity.

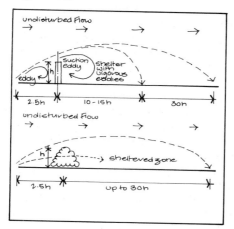

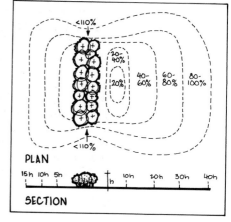

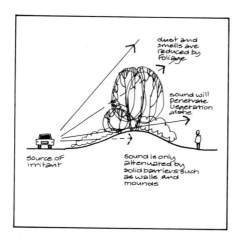

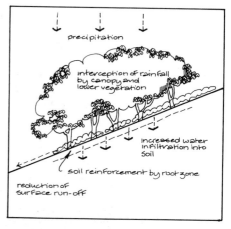

Figure 6.1   *Top left:* comparison of shelter provided by solid and perforated screens.

Figure 6.4   *Bottom left:* established vegetation significantly aids soil stability on most slopes and reduces rapid surface water run-off.

Figure 6.2   *Top right:* reduction of wind speeds obtained from shelterbelts.

Figure 6.3   *Bottom right:* vegetation can reduce local atmospheric pollution but has little value in controlling the spread of sound.

2   They take in carbon dioxide and produce oxygen, so are vital to the maintenance of the earth's atmosphere.

3   Leaf surfaces trap airborne dust and soot, and experiments have shown that the air 15m to the lee of roadside planting contains only half of the quantity of dust particles found on the windward side.

Soil Stabilization

Soil erosion can become a real problem on steeper slopes, particularly where the soil has been disturbed or replaced following construction works, or where trees have been felled. Stabilization can be achieved by the introduction of appropriate plant materials. Once established, many species provide effective protection against erosion by binding the soil surface with their roots. Grasses are particularly effective and are often used because they establish quickly and develop an extensive fibrous root system, penetrating well into the ground.

Hydraulic seeding is a technique which can be used where conventional seeding is not possible — for instance, on steep slopes. The seed is applied by hose, in a water solution. Binding materials may be applied to stabilize the surface temporarily while the seeds germinate. It may also contain organic material like chopped straw to act as a protective mulch.

Ground-cover plants which root as they spread, like ivy, periwinkle or *Rubus tricolor,* can be as effective as grass, but take longer to form a continuous cover and may not always be suitable on steep slopes. Although shrubs and ground-cover plants are more expensive than grass initially, their long-term maintenance costs are much lower than frequently mown grass and their appearance may contribute much more to the landscape.

Whilst the root systems of trees and shrubs help to bind the soil, the canopy height is also important. Low-growing shrubs can reduce the physical impact of rainfall on the soil. Conversely, the uninterrupted leaf drip from the canopy of tall trees can cause more disturbance to the soil surface than natural rainfall. It may be important, therefore, to provide some form of ground cover, in addition to trees, to reduce surface erosion on steeper slopes.

An alternative technique of stabilizing newly formed slopes is to use willow wands, which root very easily. These may be woven into mats or hurdles, which are pegged onto steep slopes where they soon root *in situ.* Alternatively, they are merely driven into the slope in rows about 300mm apart so as to create a living tree cover which can be kept low and dense by coppicing from time to time.

Figure 6.5   In hot climates, a primary function of planting is the provision of shade.

CHAPTER 7

Plant Selection

Aesthetic judgement in relation to landscape design is inevitably personal and this is particularly the case in the selection of plants.

The most important factor to consider when choosing plants is that their long-term overall form, texture and foliage colour is *generally* more significant than their short-term flower colours or autumn tints.

Form

The form of a plant refers to its overall shape and to the arrangement of its branches, leaves, buds and flowers. The natural form of plants can be influenced by external factors, such as exposure to prevailing winds, infertile soils or drought. The proximity of other plants may also have an effect. The form of a tree, for example, depends upon whether the tree grows alone in the open or as part of a group in a copse or in woodland. Where trees grow upwards in competition with each other they have much narrower crowns. Young trees and low-growing trees can also be suppressed by the shading of nearby older and larger trees.

The natural form of plants can also be influenced by landscape design techniques. Clipping to create formal hedges and create topiary can have a dramatic effect. Trees can be used to create a specific architectural form: for example, limes can be trained over metal arches to create a green tunnel – which provides shade and cool conditions on hot summer days and a fine tracery in winter.

Tree crowns can best be modified by thinning or lifting the crown whenever the canopy is too dense or too low rather than by lopping off branches which merely creates a crude caricature of a tree. It is often preferable to fell a tree that is particularly oversized for its location and to replace it with a few, more appropriate, tree species.

The basic form of trees grown in the open varies widely, from upright (fastigiate) trees such as Lombardy poplar or Italian cypress, to rounded wide-spreading deciduous trees such as oak, beech or chestnut. Similarly, shrub forms vary from the pronounced horizontal branching of *Juniperus sabina tamariscifolia* or *Viburnum plicatum 'Mariesii'*, to the vertically growing Irish juniper or bamboo. The form of plants may also vary considerably during their life cycle. The Scots pine, for instance, has a symmetrical appearance when young but becomes quite asymmetric with age, with its own distinctive and beautiful character.

The vertical, rounded and flatter forms of tree, shrubs or plants may be assembled to create either dynamic or static compositions. Broad forms suggest

Figure 7.1   The distinctive horizontal branching of *Viburnum plicatum "Maresii"* can be used to balance a composition of mixed forms.

solidity and balance and carry the eye downward or horizontally. Narrow or columnar forms attract attention, taking the eye upwards and acting as a pivotal point in a mixed grouping.

Texture

The textural character of a plant arises from the impact of all its parts – the size, shape and surface of the leaves, the way they overlap to create shadows, the nature of the leaf edges and the texture of the trunk and of the branches. Leaves may be glossy or dull, smooth or hairy, consistent or uneven. As trees mature, the texture of the bark becomes a more significant feature. For instance, the smooth bark of young black poplars gradually develops into the craggy surface seen on the older trees.

The texture of deciduous plants varies with the seasons. For example, *Buddleia* appears a relatively coarse plant during summer when it is in leaf but has a bold tracery of branches in winter. Evergreens, on the other hand, have a generally consistent texture throughout the year. The texture and colour of stems and bark becomes especially important in winter. Plants like the birches, 'whitewashed' bramble *(Rubus cockburnianus)* and the yellow- or red-stemmed dogwoods are invaluable as seasonal focal points. Trees with rugged bark when mature – for example, oak, pines, black poplars and white willows – also offer winter interest. The deeply serrated twisted trunks of sweet chestnut are also most distinctive.

The appearance of texture varies with distance. Fine textures can be appreciated at close quarters, but are less effective at a distance. The apparent mass or weight of a plant can be influenced by the reflection of light by the leaves. It is the reflective, smooth light-coloured leaves and bark of the birch which create its 'light' character. On the other hand, the horse chestnut, with its large, close, dull green leaves has a more 'solid' appearance, reinforced by the

Figure 7.2 The visual interest of this plant group relies on contrasting forms and textures, rather than flowers.

Figure 7.3 A group of bold textured plants can become the focal point of a planting design.

Figure 7.4   A well-trimmed beech hedge is a satisfying foil to this smooth piece of sculpture.

dense shadow beneath its heavy boughs. Such contrasts in texture can be used effectively. For example, birches make a pleasing foil to dark green pines or cedars or informal hedges of large shrubs such as Portuguese laurel.

The use of texture depends on the scale of a design. Large-scale planting relies upon massed effect but, in small-scale design, one sizable plant of interesting texture can become a focal point against a background of even-textured, unassuming species.

Texture is particularly important when choosing plants for prominent positions, where accent and interest arise from textural contrasts with the surroundings. An elaborate or strong foliage pattern can be used to excellent effect, seen against a fine textured background such as a yew hedge, a wall or small-leaved plants.

Evergreen shrubs with small close-textured foliage, like some of the *Berberis*, make a restrained, as well as an effective, sheltering background to other shrubs or less hardy herbaceous species.

Shiny-leaved evergreens, such as hollies or *Griselinia littoralis* enliven hedges and screen planting, but can make less suitable backgrounds to pieces of garden sculpture as they reflect light. The fine-textured, dark green, matt leaves of common yew are the ideal sculptural backdrop. An alternative might be a well-trimmed beech hedge. There can be no definite rules, however, as the form and colour of sculpture varies from polished near white marble to dull green bronze in need of enlivening.

Colour

In Britain, natural landscape colours tend to be muted. The rural landscape is composed largely of a limited range of greens, browns, and greys. Subtle seasonal contrasts are provided by flowers, fruits, autumn leaf and stem colours. The wild flowers like the poppies, cornflowers and bluebells also play their part. Widely different effects are caused by changes of light, by moisture in the air and dew held on the leaves.

In rural landscape schemes it is important to be aware of the natural colours of the landscape to ensure that new broad-scale or framework planting is in character with its surroundings. This can be achieved by confining the palette of trees and shrubs to those which thrive in the area.

Many plants have been introduced to Britain from around the world, and new cultivars and varieties have been developed in the last 150 years. So, in addition to the range of soft colours found in native British trees and shrubs, a wide selection of foliage and flower colour is available from non-native species like the ornamental maples, flowering cherries, camellias, azaleas, rhododendrons and a wide variety of conifers. Those that are overbright can create a discordant note in the rural scene.

Figure 7.5   The impact of a small group of potted plants relies on the contrast between their foliage and the geometry of the setting.

In urban planting, however, the background is seldom green. An environment of artificial colours is represented by a spectrum of bricks, masonry, concrete, and coloured claddings. In this situation, a wider range of bright plants may be quite appropriate. The greens of ordinary foliage contrast well with the city background colours and, boldly used, purple foliage can look striking against the pale colours of concrete cladding or blockwork. However the selection of plants for their colour needs to be carefully made: the same purple-leaved plants against red brickwork would look quite dull. Rendered walls painted with strong colour restrict planting choice, but the traditional white, cream or buff washes accommodate a wide range of plant colours, as well as reflecting more light back generally and on to the foliage in particular.

Colour can be modified in several ways. The amount of light reaching the plant, from full sun to shade, has a highlighting or moderating effect on colours. Subtle greys may be indistinguishable from one another in an ill-lit space. The time of day and year also affects the type and quality of light because of the variation in the intensity and angle of the sun and the humidity of the air.

The distance from which the plant is observed also affects the brightness and clarity of its colour. The 'warm' colours – reds, yellows and oranges – seem to 'advance' towards the observer, while the 'cool' blues, greens and purples appear to recede.

Strong sunlight tends to lighten colours and this effect can be heightened by using the 'warm' shades in the sun and the 'cool' colours in the shade. White or pale flowers are also valuable for brightening shaded areas and lightening the colour values on dull days, at dawn and at dusk.

Colour should always be used in large enough areas, relative to the scale of the scheme to read clearly. The use of too many colours tends to create discord, so the transition from colour to colour should be gradual, except where strong colour contrasts are the aim of the composition.

Figure 7.6   Contrasts in texture and form can be quite subtle as in this informal setting.

Figure 7.7 Strong sunlight lightens colours and heightens the contrast of light and shade.

Colour also helps to define spaces and can give a special character to individual spaces, as in the orange and red or the blue and white 'outdoor rooms' at Hidcote, each enclosed by dark green hedges. Sylvia Crowe in *Garden Design* suggests three successful ways of designing with colour:

'One is the Italian method of designing a picture in monotone, enlivened only with high notes of colour. The second is to observe the laws of nature, while the third, the hardest of all, is to treat the colour of plants as if they were the colours on a palette and paint pictures with them.' (p.112)

In the second method, two main opportunities need to be considered in observing the laws of nature. One is whether to use seasonal colour change as the principle of the design, relying on a range of similar colours in harmony with each other extending over a large area to give a broad effect. For example, the browns, reds, oranges and yellows of autumn contrast strongly with the soft greens, yellows and whites of spring, although neither are seen together. The alternative is to use strong areas of single colours to provide a vivid, perhaps startling, but nevertheless controlled visual effect. The bluebell wood is an obvious example in nature, but continued effects using drifts of single colour can be equally effective in designed landscapes.

With the third method – using colours on a palette and painting pictures with them – can prove very difficult in practice to achieve satisfactory results. Geometric patterns are perhaps the easiest way of using this method, the Elizabethan knot garden or herb garden being typical examples. Burle Marx applied a philosophy of abstraction, contemporary with other parallels in modern art, to create stunning effects. However, to be successful, this type of design requires a very detailed knowledge of plants, their flower colours and their seasonal variations, and an excellent grasp of colour relationships. Careful and continuous management control is necessary to maintain such planting designs, and costs are on the high side.

Planting schemes should generally be designed to provide interest throughout the year. Variety in foliage through the seasons can be achieved by a mix of deciduous and evergreen plants. The colour of evergreen foliage does not change significantly with the seasons but, at close quarters, the flush of new conifer needles, or the midsummer appearance of fresh new leaves on evergreen shrubs, adds greatly to their interest. In contrast, the foliage of deciduous plants changes markedly with the seasons, from the fresh, light colours of spring through the darker, heavier shades of summer to autumn tints. Coloured or variegated foliage widens the scope of colour design, since it is present for a longer period than flowers or fruit.

Foliage colours available, other than the many shades of green, are reds, purples, bronzes, yellows, silvers and felted greys. Autumn colours can be quite dramatic, although in Britain their duration is often truncated by autumn gales.

Against a dark background, variegated or light-coloured leaves or needles show up well, and evergreen shrubs with coloured foliage can provide important year-round interest. Dark and shady areas can be brightened by plants with glossy-leaves and variegated foliage.

Flowers provide welcome areas of interest in a composition. Flowering periods vary greatly in their duration from one species to another. Some species, such as brooms, have only one short flowering period while others, like perpetual roses or *Potentillas*, produce flowers over a long season or flower intermittently. Species without other attractions, selected only for their flowers, should be used sparingly.

Fruit and berries can be an important feature in the autumn. The red and orange berries of plants such as *Cotoneaster* and *Pyracantha* and the pink and white berries of *Pernettya* and *Symphoricarpos* can be used to great effect. The persistent fruits of many plants are not only visually attractive but also encourage wildlife, especially birds, throughout the winter. Rose hips, the berries of *Cotoneasters*, *Pyracanthas* and the *Berberis* family and the fruits of the crab

Figure 7.8 A mix of evergreen and deciduous plants will provide foliage interest throughout the year.

Plate 1   The autumnal colour of a climbing vine softens and frames this doorway.

Plate 2 Green is a visually restful colour and creates a relaxing ambiance when combined with standing water.

Plate 3 Herbaceous plants provide interesting contrasts of colour and texture both in leaf and flower.

Plate 4 The traditional English display of herbaceous plants, in a border backed by a tall hedge.

Plate 5 An imaginative use of violas to create a cascade of colour. (Stoke on Trent Garden Festival)

Plate 6   Formal tree planting can create grand outdoor rooms.

Plate 7   The light and shade cast beneath a pergola.

Figure 7.9   The brilliant winter colours of Dogwood bark are encouraged by annual hard pruning in the spring.

apples and rowans are typical examples of winter food sources.

Bark colours come into their own in winter, particularly the bright reds and yellows of the dogwoods and willows. Dense growth of coloured stems is encouraged by annual hard pruning of these shrubs in the spring. Paper-bark birch and some of the maples and smaller cherries also have distinctive bark and provide effective focal points if sited against a darker foil to catch the low winter sun.

Scent

Many shrubs, and some trees have pleasantly scented flowers or foliage, making them especially appreciated when planted by paths, seats, doorways, and close to groundfloor windows. They are particularly welcomed by blind or partially sighted people and there is an advantage in planting them in raised beds, so making the scent more readily appreciated.

Sound

There are a few plants whose foliage makes a very characteristic sound in the slightest breeze – for instance, aspen trees, bamboos, and tall grasses such as *Miscanthus sinensis*. They add a new dimension of interest, particularly for those unable to see.

The next six chapters examine the main classes of plant material in greater depth before returning to overall questions of management and supply. This is followed by a final chapter on Woodlands which is, at the same time, an overview of how an integrated landscape approach working with, rather than against, nature, can make the greatest contribution to a better landscape.

CHAPTER 8

Trees

Trees and Buildings

Sylvia Crowe expressed the significance of trees in the landscape very successfully: 'Trees should be looked upon as a gift to any site, and no felling be done without long thought and strong reasons' *(Garden Design* p.162).

Although developers may claim that they prefer to work on a completely cleared site for economic reasons, existing trees are now becoming more widely recognized as a valuable visual asset to any development. Mature existing trees provide a sense of scale, which even the faster-growing new trees cannot attain for a number of decades.

In order to be in a position to decide which trees and shrubs should be retained, an accurate tree survey and arboricultural assessment of the existing trees should be carried out before site-planning commences. At the same time the designers should take account of any restrictions of tree-felling, such as trees within Conservation Areas or those covered by Tree Preservation Orders.

The extent of root systems is difficult to gauge, because their development is unpredictable even in consistent soil conditions. Feeder roots grow most strongly in the direction of the more fertile soil and best water supply, while anchor roots develop in response to the direction of the prevailing wind. As a rule-of-thumb for assessing the risk of root damage, it is reasonable to assume that the root system spreads at least several metres beyond the edge of the canopy. However, with some trees, such as poplars, the root spread is generally substantially greater than the spread of the canopy.

Maintaining mature trees in a reasonably healthy condition requires several factors to be taken into account early in the design process.

Ground levels

When retaining trees, ground levels should remain virtually unchanged within the spread of their canopy to prevent damage to the surface feeder roots. Some species can tolerate a modest increase of levels, up to about 75mm, depending on their age. If the ground level has to be raised, it should be done gradually over several years using light porous soil. Since a large proportion of roots occur in the top 700–1000mm of soil, raising the ground level progressively reduces the amount of air reaching the roots. Clearly, any more than a modest amount of excavation within this zone could result in significant loss of anchor and feeder roots. Trees can be retained above new ground levels by constructing, if necessary, low retaining walls beyond the edge of the canopy. However, they may still be adversely affected by a lowering of the water table. Advice on this should be sought from an arboriculturalist who could also assess the potential value of artificial irrigation.

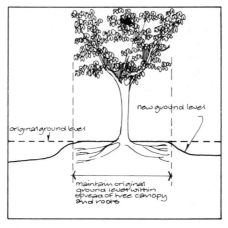

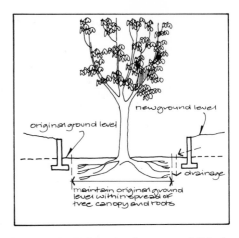

Figure 8.1   Preferable method of reducing ground levels around established trees.

Figure 8.2   Raising levels near established trees.

The water table

New developments frequently alter the water table, endangering the lives of existing trees. Some species, such as oaks, are more susceptible than others. A mature tree may be unable to adapt quickly enough to maintain an adequate water supply for its canopy when the water table is lowered. This problem can sometimes be alleviated by reducing the canopy by crown thinning. This is a skilled job, to be carried out by a qualified arboriculturalist. It is essential to ensure that the crown is carefully thinned to retain its natural shape, rather than being disfigured by lopping or topping.

Where the water table is raised, the roots of existing trees may be deprived of oxygen, causing them to slowly die. Land drains, laid close to the tree's roots and connected to the surface drainage system, can help to alleviate this problem.

Roots and underground services

Conflicts between existing trees and proposed services tend to arise when there is a lack of coordination between the consultants at a sufficiently early stage in the design process. Where a tree is to be retained, the path of underground services should avoid its root spread altogether, bearing in mind that the amenity value of mature trees far exceeds the cost of a few manholes or metres of cable. Where the services cannot be diverted around the roots they should be threaded between roots by hand.

If roots are cut, the health and stability of the tree will be affected, particularly if they are cut extensively. Roots larger than 70mm diameter should not be cut, and all those over 25mm diameter cut as sparingly as possible. If large roots have to be severed, they must be cut cleanly and treated with a fungicidal dressing to minimize the risk of infection. Arboricultural advice should be sought on the possibility of compensating for root loss by thinning the tree canopy so that the water loss from the crown is reduced.

Roots and foundations

Shrinkable clay soils expand and contract seasonally as the soil moisture level increases in the autumn and decreases in the spring when trees take up soil water, so causing soil shrinkage. Where a tree is felled on a development site, the mass of clay, corresponding roughly with its root system, slowly expands. Unless adequate precautions are taken, this expansion can damage the structure of buildings so the foundations of new buildings or walls close to existing trees on shrinkable clays should extend down to a level below that at which soil shrinkage occurs. Alternatively, the building may be built on groundbeams supported by piles. The foundations of freestanding brick walls can be bridged locally across a trees' roots.

Paving

Feeder roots running just beneath the ground surface frequently cause paving slabs to lift irregularly and the cracking of hard surfaces, like asphalt, as well as walls with poor foundations. This problem is best averted by using porous surfacing such as gravel around trees in paved areas.

New impervious paving over established tree roots eventually kills trees by depriving them of air and water. To prevent this, an area of open surfacing, such as gravel, loose-laid cobbles or perforated paving units should be laid around the bole of existing trees and as much of the area under the canopy spread as is practicable. Metal tree grilles could be used, but would be very expensive in this situation. They are more appropriate for use with newly planted trees.

Protection

It is essential to protect trees adequately during construction. Stout fencing should be erected one metre beyond the edge of the canopy of the tree, or group of trees, to protect the root system while building and civil engineering work is in progress. No temporary huts, stored materials, or any type of vehicles should be allowed within the canopy spread, or fires lit within 10 metres of the canopy edge. As earthmoving machines can compact topsoil and crush surface roots in a single pass, they should not be allowed to manoeuvre amongst existing trees.

Damage to trunks and branches by machines and vehicles is all too common on building sites. Penalty clauses in contracts should reflect the aesthetic and economic value placed upon individual trees to discourage damage, and clear, unambiguous instructions to the contractor are essential to warn him of his liability. As a precaution, the contractor can be required to deposit a bond, to be

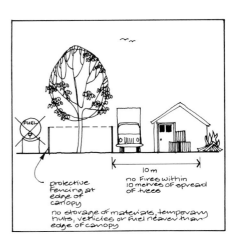

Figure 8.3 Protective measures for trees on development sites.

held in a joint account, for the replacement of damaged trees, if necessary. There must, however, be provision for arbitration by an agreed party. Minor damage should be dealt with immediately by cutting back to clean wood to minimize fungal infection.

Felling

Where trees grow together, their root and branch systems tend to interlock, so that it is often difficult to remove one tree from a group without the others being adversely affected. Moreover, when one tree is removed, roots of the others may be cut, making them prone to wind damage.

Where felled trees are to be completely removed, they are normally cut off close to ground level and the stumps uprooted to prevent regrowth by side shoots or suckering and fungal infection which may then spread to nearby trees. Stumps may be removed by bulldozer, or they can be cut down below ground level by a stump grinder or chipper. The stump can also be killed by chemicals applied into drill holes. However, in amenity woodland, the stumps are best left to decay *in situ* as they provide a habitat for a wide range of flora and fauna.

Planting trees near buildings

Potential problems include light obstruction, leaves blocking gutters, slippery conditions underfoot due to decaying leaves left on paving, obstruction of overhead cables, and damage by roots to foundations and underground drains.

These problems can be minimized if due consideration is given to the ultimate height, spread and canopy density of the trees chosen. Only those trees with a light leaf canopy, like ash, rowan or birch, should be planted near buildings, as they allow more light through than those with dense, large leaves, like horse chestnut. Where trees are proposed to screen buildings from the sun's glare, they should be planted sufficiently far away from windows to take account of their eventual size. Deciduous trees are more appropriate than evergreens in this situation, since they let through substantially more light in winter than in summer.

Certain trees, including poplars and willows, require more water than others. On shrinkable clay soils these species can cause problems to building foundations and to drains. Tiny roots can penetrate cracks in mortar-jointed clay drains and grow into them. The crack widens as the roots grow, and the interior of the drain may soon become blocked. Fortunately, the widespread use of drains with rubber or plastic sealing rings helps to reduce this problem.

Existing trees growing close to overhead lines must be pruned to maintain clearance. Service authorities, such as Electricity Boards, have the right to prune them if the owners do not keep the branches certain specified distances away from the power lines. This conflict can be avoided by planting some distance away, and the service authorities can provide advice on required clearances.

Trees growing near buildings, or in urban areas, may also give cause for concern through the danger of falling branches. However, most healthy trees are unlikely to suffer such problems and, if inspected regularly, the potential risk can be monitored and remedial action can be taken when necessary.

Trees and Roads in the Countryside

Roadside planting is a specialized subject. Trees are important in integrating roads with their surroundings and linking urban areas with the countryside.

They can act as a psychological baffle against the distraction of traffic and absorb dust arising from traffic or industrial processes.

Roadside planting should reflect the likely speed of movement. Small, regularly spaced groups or individual trees should be avoided, as they can be very trying visually and may even induce a mild hypnotic effect. Planting in irregular groups can help to overcome this problem. Tree groups used to create solid masses or mixed woodland, carefully sited to contrast with open areas, or framing views can help to relieve the monotony of driving down long, straight roads over flat landscapes.

Highway planting must not interfere with sight lines along the road or at junctions. Where development schemes affect public highways, or roads which the local authority is expected to maintain, the landscape proposals should comply with the highway authority's detailed design requirements.

Trees in Towns

Trees are a great asset in streets and urban squares, especially where there is sufficient space for the larger species to grow freely into mature trees.

Urban spaces devoid of trees tend to be barren and depressing. Given proper landscape planning trees can be successfully incorporated into virtually every urban land use, from commercial, office and mixed developments, to housing and industrial sites. The choice of tree should relate to the use of the space and its appropriateness in terms of size and character. Forest trees should not be

Figure 8.4   Trees are a great asset in urban squares, especially where there is sufficient space for the larger species to grow to maturity.

Figure 8.5   Street trees and other vegetation benefit from sufficient growing space and adequate drainage.

Figure 8.6   Well situated trees will close vistas and soften exposed edges of building composition.

Figure 8.7   Trees are particularly valued in car parks for their welcome shade in summer.

Figure 8.8 Trees in an urban setting softening the visual impact of both a car park and buildings.

planted in narrow city streets where they will eventually have to be lopped or pollarded. Instead, columnar or conical cultivars of larger trees, such as the fastigiate hornbeam, may be selected in preference to smaller, round-crowned specimens such as crab apples or hawthorns, which may not relate satisfactorily to the scale of taller buildings.

Although street trees are often planted in rows, where there is insufficient space, small groups at the end of closed streets or between car parking bays can effectively punctuate the street scene.

Trees in Car Parks

Surface car parks are often the most visually instrusive aspect of modern developments. They are frequently unscreened and so diminish the quality of the surrounding area. This is especially apparent in summer, when sunlight reflects off the parked vehicles. Tree planting can ameliorate this effect. A tree screen on the perimeter of the car park helps to integrate it with its surroundings and the trees planted within the car park itself reduce the impact of hard surfaces and vehicles. They also provide welcome shade in summer, wind shelter in winter and can be used to give a distinctive character to the different sections of large car parks. To control glare from shiny metal and glass, the trees should be planted to develop an overlapping canopy of foliage in summer and provide continuous shading on southerly facing aspects. Grid layouts for tree planting are ordered and provide a unifying element in even the most dismal of car parks. Where the site is irregular, grouping trees at strategic points may be visually more attractive and more practical. In any event, a few odd trees, scattered more or less indiscrimately throughout a large car park, are unlikely to provide effective relief.

Trees selected for car parks must be able to tolerate generally hostile growing conditions: drought, reflected heat and glare from surfaces together with leaking oil and exhaust fumes. The trunks must be protected from accidental damage and this may be achieved by using raised beds, kerbs, rails or bollards. The trunks of larger specimen trees planted in hard surfaced areas can benefit from being wrapped in hessian for the first few years, to reduce overheating.

Limes and sycamores suffer from aphid attack which gives rise to unpleasant sticky deposits, and they should therefore not be planted in car parks. Chestnuts have a heavy leaf fall which may lead to skidding and accidents. The large leaves also make clearance a more difficult problem.

Trees in the Countryside

Since the 1970s, Dutch Elm disease and changing farm techniques have caused many trees to be felled. The majority have not been replaced, so the rural landscape has changed dramatically in some areas. The natural regeneration of individual trees in the countryside has also been substantially reduced by the unselective use of hedge-trimming machines. When hedges were cared for by hand, trees growing up through them could easily be selectively retained.

As a result of these changes, the replacement of trees in the countryside is now far more dependent on deliberate planting. The value to the farmer of trees around fields depends upon the type of agriculture being practised. Perhaps as a result of agricultural set-aside, greater consideration can now be given to new woodland planting. Where sheep and cattle are reared traditionally, shelter and shade for them are still important, particularly in exposed upland areas. The increasing practice of overwintering stock in sheds or covered yards reduces the need to plant field shelter belts for their protection but has changed the emphasis to sheltering the farm buildings themselves, particularly where they are exposed to winter winds.

Trees around arable fields may not be favoured by farmers because they compete with crops by shading them to a limited extent on the north side, making them slower to germinate and ripen. However, this is compensated by better growth to the south of the trees due to earlier soil warming, the balance between the factors being a matter of local circumstances.

Many farmers who have removed hedges and trees in the interests of agricultural efficiency are sensitive to the broader landscape value of trees on their land and have since replanted along ownership boundaries and roadsides, by gateways and in field corners. The Forestry Commission and Countryside Commission, as well as some county or district councils, offer grant-aid to encourage the planting of tree groups and small deciduous woodlands in the countryside. Advice may also be given to landowners on tree planting and management.

Trees are planted in the countryside for a wide variety of non-agricultural reasons. As a result of increasing pressure from the environmentally-conscious public for new developments to include tree planting, it is often required as a condition of planning consent. Trees and shrubs, chosen to reflect the species growing around the site, can help to integrate new works into the existing landscape pattern.

Figure 8.9 Loss of trees during the 20th century has changed much of lowland, rural Britain dramatically and few areas remain that are as well wooded as this.

CHAPTER 9

Shrubs and Hedges

Shrubs

A wide variety of shrubs are used in landscape design – evergreen and deciduous, native and exotic – the selection of shrubs for a scheme being often very much a personal choice. However, native species which are adapted to the climate and soils of the British Isles should be used in preference to more exotic species, especially where the new planting is also to provide a habitat or a food source for wildlife. Many plant species are highly adaptable and so can be used successfully in a wide range of situations.

The production of nursery grown stock depends partly on the ability of nurseries to meet demands from designers for the supply of particular species. The Joint Council for Landscape Industries has tried to assist this process by producing a list of plant material, including shrubs, commonly produced and commonly specified. In this way, designers are less likely to specify plants which are not grown and nurseries are less likely to produce plants which are not generally specified. The list also assists in identifying the range of sizes at which the plants are generally available. The list is aimed at amenity landscape work rather than the garden centre industry.

Plants which are commonly used in landscape work come from a relatively small range of families and genera. The most widely used family in landscape design is the *Rosaceae*, which includes many flowering and fruit-producing evergreen and deciduous trees and shrubs. Within this family are *Amelanchiers*, *Cotoneasters*, hawthorns, *Kerrias*, apples, cherries, *Potentillas*, *Pyracanthas*, *Spireas*, rowans and whitebeams as well as the rose family itself. Another very useful family in landscape design are the Legumes. Many species in this family have the ability to fix nitrogen in the soil and can therefore be particularly useful in reclamation work on poor and 'truncated' soils. Within this family the following species are commonly used – brooms, *Genistas*, gorse, *Robinia* and *Gleditsia*.

The *Ericaceae* family includes many plants that are acid-tolerant, such as heaths and heathers, rhododendrons and azaleas and *Pernettyas* and *Pieris*. Other families are the *Berberidaceae* which include *Berberis* and *Mahonia*; the *Eleagnaceae*, which includes *Eleagnus*, and sea buckthorn; the *Oleaceae*, which include privets and *Osmanthus*, and the *Labiatae*, which include herbs such as lavender, rosemary and thyme.

The mature size of the shrubs selected should be related to the proportions of the spaces they define, enclose or subdivide. Their colours, seasonal changes and textures should be an integral part of the design, as well as reflecting the inherent characteristics of the site.

To achieve the maximum visual effect in large schemes, shrubs are best planted in massed groups of a single species, to create a significant impact. From a practical viewpoint, it is better to plant shrubs in bold, informal groups in good-sized beds rather than as individual plants in grass. Maintenance of shrub beds is simplified if they are laid out in circular or free-flowing shapes, without corners. In paved spaces, like a courtyard, a single large shrub can make an ideal focal point. Evergreens have particular value here – for example, the sweet-scented *Osmanthus*, *Ceanothus* or *Viburnum*.

Maintenance

Many shrubs require regular pruning, to retain a compact form, encourage flowering and maintain vigour. The exact timing and nature of pruning depends on individual species. Some shrubs, like the yellow- and red-stemmed willows and dogwoods, need annual cutting back as only the young growth is vividly coloured.

Hedges

The success of a hedge depends on matching the species with the design function and subsequent maintenance. A hedge intended as a screen must achieve the necessary height and density, while a barrier hedge should be thorny, vigorous and capable of regeneration after damage. The speed with which plants reach their required height and spread is an important factor in making a final selection.

The character of a hedge is influenced by the type and frequency of maintenance. If regular maintenance cannot be assured, it is better to plan for

Figure 9.1   This low lavender hedge is sufficient to define the boundary of a formal space.

Figure 9.2 Shrubs are best planted in bold, informal groups, in beds of free-flowing form.

an informal hedge using, for example, varieties of *Berberis*, *Pyracantha* or *Rosa rugosa*.

The choice of species and maintenance techniques should also be appropriate to the situation. For example, native species are suitable for rural areas and clipped or flowering hedges might be selected for towns.

The relationship between the scale of the enclosed space and the surrounding hedges should be carefully considered. Visual interest and vertical scale can be added by allowing selected saplings to mature into hedgerow trees or by including standard trees amongst the hedge planting.

Within a garden or a larger space, hedges can be used as the main formal elements to delineate spaces of different proportions and geometry. Finally, hedges may be clipped to ornamental shapes and many examples of topiary can be seen in Britain. Tall formal hedges can help to link scattered buildings in much the same way that walls might be used. Dwarf hedges can also be used ornamentally, to create a surface pattern or parterre.

In the countryside, the network of hedges creates a bold landscape pattern and helps to impart a strong sense of unity to the rural scene. Hedges can therefore be an important means of integrating new developments into an existing rural landscape.

Figure 9.3   Dwarf hedges used to create a parterre.

On light soils and upland or coastal areas exposed to the wind, hedges can help to reduce soil erosion by deflecting the wind, thereby reducing its power to carry topsoil particles away. Hedges can also be effective in slowing down soil erosion caused by excessive run-off on slopes.

Rural hedges may be many centuries old, the number of species of hedge plants, herbs and animals associated with them usually increasing with age. Ancient hedgerows should be preserved for their ecological value, as well as their importance as visual and cultural features in the landscape.

Hedges are also important wildlife 'corridors', linking together woodlands, copses and ponds over large tracts of land. The smaller animals and insects with limited ability to cross open spaces can colonize new areas via these hedge routes. Hedgerows are refuges for herbaceous plants and insects away from the herbicides and pesticides applied to much agricultural land. To provide optimum wildlife habitats, new hedge planting should comprise a diversity of species.

Planting

Hedging plants are generally planted at only 450–600mm high because they establish more reliably, grow more quickly and are cheaper than larger plants. Close planting encourages upward, competitive growth and the establishment of a dense mass of leaves and twigs at an early stage.

They are normally set out in a staggered, double row, in well cultivated ground. Certain rural hedging traditions may, however, demand different treatment. For example, a Cornish hedge which is essentially an earth-filled stone wall, has its plant material established between turfs on top of the wall.

Where a hedge is likely to be trampled or is required to provide security during establishment, it may be reinforced with an appropriate fence between the two rows of plants. Agricultural hedges may require temporary fencing on both sides for initial protection against grazing. This must be set out about one metre beyond the plants.

Figure 9.4　An interesting textural effect achieved by combining hedges of different leaf sizes.

Maintenance

During the first two years or so, the plants require weeding, watering and firming in after disturbance by high winds. Once established, trimming is essential for the development of a dense hedge. If left untrimmed, a hedge will grow up and become thin and open at the bottom. The cross-section of a hedge should be wider at the base than at the top, which encourages dense growth at the base and is structurally more stable. The method of trimming depends on the character of the hedge, rather than on the species.

Formal hedges Small-leaved evergreens, beech and hornbeam can be clipped with hand-shears or electric hedge-trimmers. Light annual trimming is often all that is required to keep slower-growing species, such as yew, from expanding outside their allotted space, while some fast-growing shrubs, such as privet, need to be cut back several times each year to retain a formal shape.

Informal hedges The character of informal hedges derives largely from the shapes of the plants included in the hedge. Regular, close-pruning would destroy the informality. Occasional pruning of older shoots to encourage flowering or new growth is all that is generally required.

Figure 9.5   This example of topiary has an unusually abstract sculptural form.

Figure 9.7 *Above:* Rural hedges are important wildlife 'corridors' linking woodland, copses and streams.

Figure 9.6 *Below:* Preferred hedge profiles.

Rural hedges In the past, stockproof hedges of mixed species were traditionally maintained by laying. With this method, most of the hedge is cut back, while selected shoots are retained and partly cut through near the base. They are then bent to lie almost horizontally, interlaced and secured with vertical timber stakes, at about 1.0m intervals. In effect, the hedge is converted into a living, stockproof fence. This is an expensive, highly-skilled and labour-intensive operation, but it only needs to be done at intervals of 8–10 years, depending on the species and location.

Being only a fraction of the cost of skilled hedge-laying, hedge-trimming, carried out with a tractor-mounted mechanical flail, is more commonly practised but, to be successful, it needs to be carried out carefully. More often, it produces a hedge which is coarse in appearance. If it is carried out indiscriminately, it destroys the young trees, some of which the traditional hedge-layer would have left to grow up as hedgerow trees. It is possible to identify specific young trees within a hedge that ought to be retained. Many years of indiscriminate treatment can result in a crudely-cut, unbalanced hedge, which is no longer stockproof because it becomes more sparse near ground level. It also becomes devalued as a wildlife habitat being less dense and less sheltering.

CHAPTER 10

Climbers and Wall Shrubs

In urban situations, climbers can be used on buildings, walls or fences, where there is little space for more substantial planting. They can also be planted in containers on roofs, access decks and balconies so as to drape downwards. Climbers on building façades can provide some protection from weathering. Visually, they can help to relate buildings to the adjacent landscape spaces.

Because some climbers, like the Russian vine, grow extremely fast, they are invaluable for providing screening or hiding unsightly structures relatively quickly. The fastest-growing climbers are deciduous. Where foliage is required all the year round, both slow-growing evergreen and fast-growing deciduous species may be planted together. In some situations, it may be appropriate to plant annual climbers for an immediate effect.

Pergolas or other outdoor structures can be covered with climbers to provide shade, colour and scent. Many materials, such as timber or metal, can be used for these structures, perhaps combined with brick or stone piers. Their forms range from simple post and beam structures, cantilevered beams projecting from a building, to more complex freestanding pergolas which are designed as a focal point in a composition. The overhead structural elements may be large and solid, or slender and delicate. The visual success of a structure depends on its scale in relation to the other components in the design.

Most climbers do not harm the structure of a building or wall. However ivy which is a self-clinging creeper, can damage brickwork which is already in poor repair by entering open joints and further loosening weak mortar. Climbers provide a habitat for a variety of wildlife, especially roosting and nesting sites for birds.

Growth Habit

Climbers fall into three general groups, each with a distinct growing habit.

Creepers

These are self-clinging climbers which do not require a support. Ivy and climbing hydrangea (*Hydrangea petiolaris*) attach themselves with aerial rootlets, while Virginia creeper and Boston ivy adhere to surfaces by means of small tendrils or sucker pads. These climbers should not be used on a painted wall or fence, since it is difficult to gain access later without cutting the plants back. Because self-clinging climbers are often reluctant to start to cling by themselves, they initially need a cane support.

Twisters and twiners

Twisting, climbing plants coil their stems around supports; honeysuckle and wisteria being typical examples. Other plants develop tendrils which twine around a support, examples of these being vines and the passion flower. Both types of plant need supporting structures, such as trellis, or wires. Climbers with a twisting habit will also grow on open fences and pergolas. Trees can also support climbers, but could be smothered by vigorous climbers if they are not controlled.

Wall shrubs

Wall shrubs include rambling roses, *Pyracanthas* and trained fruit trees. Generally, they are only partially self-supporting so their stems need to be artificially attached to wires or trellises as they develop. A greater amount of maintenance is necessary than for climbers. Some need annual pruning to encourage flowering and wall fruit trees need considerable attention in the early years, to form an espalier or fan shape and to encourage fruit formation.

Many wall shrubs are bulky when mature and therefore need to be planted with enough space to allow for future growth. Those with woody and inflexible stems should only be used against walls or fences with little need for maintenance access.

Figure 10.1   Self-clinging climbers, such as Virginia Creeper, are invaluable for their ability to cover large areas unaided.

Figure 10.2 Self-clinging climbers can provide additional interest to unusual architectural forms.

Figure 10.3   Climbers can be trained to form architectural features, such as this tunnel of Laburnum.

Supports

Unless the supporting structure is a design feature in its own right, like a pergola, it should be neat and inconspicuous. Lines of wires spaced 200–300mm apart, metal grids, or timber trellis are all suitable. The latter can, if stoutly supported by posts, be freestanding. The choice should depend on the colour and character of the background. For walls or fences wires can be secured to hardened steel nails with lead clips, driven in until about 10mm is protruding. A better method is to thread the wires through galvanized vine eyes, driven or screwed into the supporting structure. The wires may be tensioned with adjustable devices, if they are strongly anchored at both ends.

Where climbers are planted against a surface that needs regular maintenance, a non-clinging species with flexible stems should be used, such as honeysuckle. This may be supported on an easily removable trellis hung on hooks screwed into the fence or wall. When plants are supported on wooden structures care must be taken to ensure that they do not come into contact with fresh timber preservatives, which can scorch and kill the foliage.

All external structures should be designed to take account of snow and wind loads, *including* the desired canopy of foliage, as they may have to resist considerable forces, especially in exposed locations.

Planting

There are species of climbers suitable for almost all soils, site conditions and aspects, but correct orientation is important. Some are unsuited to east-facing walls, because they are damaged by the heat of the morning sun on tissue still frozen by overnight frosts. Others, such as clematis, require a sunny situation in order to flower, but require a cool and shaded root run, in a rich, moist soil. Ground-cover plants around the foot of the climber and a heavy mulch can help to provide these conditions. A few plants will tolerate a northerly aspect. These include common ivy, Virginia creeper and the climbing hydrangea.

Climbers should normally be planted about 200–300mm away from walls, to avoid the dry conditions above the foundations. Climbers grown over pergolas or on trellises should be planted on the windward side of the structure. Many climbers tend to produce most of their flowers on the south side of the plant. The selection of plants and the orientation of walls, pergolas or other supporting structures should take account of these factors.

The foot of a wall is generally a hostile environment for plants. Soils which are poor and dry should be improved by the addition of manure or compost at the time of planting. Climbers benefit from mulching and the annual application of fertilizer.

Figure 10.4 The flowers of climbing roses provide additional interest whilst breaking up the mass of walls.

CHAPTER 11

Ground Cover

'Ground cover' is the term commonly used for shrubby or herbaceous plants, up to about 600mm high, which provide a low-growing carpet. They are planted with the intention of creating a complete ground cover, when fully established, which looks attractive throughout the year. The time taken to achieve this depends on the initial size of the plants, their vigour, their planting centres and the way they are maintained. The normal design objective is that the plants should be capable of achieving complete cover within two or, at most three years. Planting centres vary considerably between species. For instance, if the species is slow-growing or is planted small, as many as 15–20 plants may be required per square metre. For example, bugle *(Ajuga reptans)* needs to be closely planted in large quantities, whereas a single pot-grown specimen of a prostrate juniper will cover a large area. Although planting at close centres may be expensive it soon leads to the benefit of reduced maintenance.

Biennials and annuals can also be used as ground cover, either directly seeded or as bedding plants. However, they are very labour-intensive, the effects are short-lived and consequently their use is rarely cost-effective.

Ground-cover plants are more appropriate than grass in situations where soft landscape is required and where mower access is difficult. Small areas of soft landscape will generally be more economic to maintain as ground cover or shrub-planting than grass, although the initial costs will be higher. Grass-cutting can be carried out with greater ease if groups of trees, bollards or signs are located in ground-cover planting. In the shade of buildings or trees they are easier to maintain than grass.

A limited palette of ground-cover plants between trees, shrubs and other elements like paths, walls and signs, is a good way of creating continuity and so achieving a degree of visual unity. Interesting textures and colours can be used without losing this effect. To retain the 'carpet' effect throughout the year, evergreen plants are frequently selected as the major ground-cover component. They can be enlivened by flowering bulbs, corms and rhizomes, whose dying foliage is soon concealed by the ground cover. In fact, this represents a more natural way of using this type of plant material.

The growth habit of ground-cover plants is very important and forms the basis for their classification:

1   Thicket formers – that is, low shrubs whose shoots form dense masses of even height. Examples: *Berberis candida* and *Rosa Max Graf.*
2   Prostrate or spreading evergreen shrubs, having horizontal or arching branches, so that each plant eventually occupies a good deal of ground, the dense foliage successfully shading out most weeds. Examples: the prostrate junipers and *Cotoneasters.*

Figure 11.1   *Above:* A dense ground cover is an effective means of shading out weeds between larger plants and trees.

Figure 11.2   *Right:* The prostrate *Cotoneasters* are successful ground coverers.

Figure 11.3   Ivy is an attractively uniform ground cover which is most tolerant of dense shade.

3   Hummock-formers which form dense low clumps that slowly increase in size. The individual plants need to be planted close together in order to form a dense carpet. Examples: heathers, *Pernettya, Iberis.*

4   Carpeting plants which spread by means of underground shoots or surface runners which root as they grow. These can be invasive on certain soils and should only be used where sufficient labour is available to control them. Examples: deadnettle, Rose of Sharon and periwinkle.

5   Clump-forming herbaceous perennial plants which tend to spread slowly. They should be planted at close centres – that is 10–15cm. Examples: *Epimediums* and *Bergenias.*

6   Climbers which are fast-growing, with long shoots can make effective, rapid cover over large areas. Some species, like honeysuckle, can be encouraged to take root by pegging down the new shoots. Others, like ivy, root readily where their shoots touch the ground. When ivy is required for ground cover, varieties with a prostrate growth habit — for example, the Irish ivy *(Hedera helix hibernica)* — should be selected, to minimize invasion of nearby shrubs and trees.

Ground-cover plants should be maintained from the outset with the objective of covering the ground quickly. Since they may be small when planted, the main problem during establishment is weed competition. Perennial weeds should be thoroughly eradicated before planting. It is difficult to hoe or apply herbicides between the closely-spaced ground-cover plants, Damage can be caused to herbaceous species by using the wrong type of herbicide or too strong a solution and users should follow makers' directions with care.

CHAPTER 12

Herbaceous Plants and Bulbs

Herbaceous plants have non-woody stems and many die back to ground level in winter. They include annuals, such as nasturtiums, which germinate, flower and die in a single season; biennials, like wallflowers, which germinate, flower and die in two seasons; and perennials, such as peony, iris, lilies and phlox, whose rootstocks are perpetual. A few perennials are evergreens, such as *Bergenia* and *Phormium*, but most are deciduous, like delphiniums.

Herbaceous plants with food storage organs, — tubers or rhizomes — are able to survive out of the ground during the dormant period. Frost-tender plants such as dahlias or begonias should be lifted and stored over winter in a cool, dark, frost-free place.

The main disadvantage of most herbaceous plants is the amount of maintenance that they require beyond routine weeding. Generally, perennials with rootstocks should be lifted and divided every two or three years, to maintain dense, vigorous growth. Dead stems need to be cut back, dead flowerheads removed and tall species with weak stems, like delphiniums, require staking. Annuals and biennials, of course, need replacing every one or two years, either from seed or with young plants.

Whilst the majority of 'bulbous' plants — that is, true bulbs, like tulips and daffodils, plants from corms, like crocus, and plants from rhizomes, like iris - flower during spring, some are summer- and autumn-flowering, and so can be used to provide a succession of flower colour throughout the year.

Design

The herbaceous border orginated in the cottage garden, where plants for food, decoration and medicinal purposes had long been grown together in an informal manner. During the nineteenth century, Gertrude Jekyll and others applied new colour design concepts to herbaceous borders, producing some magnificent designs. By the early 1900s herbaceous planting had become a popular garden feature. Unfortunately, the artistic genius which made Gertrude Jekyll borders exciting was largely lost in less thoughtful repetition.

Herbaceous borders require intensive work to keep them in good heart and so their popularity has since declined as cultural changes have given priority to lower maintenance.

Today, designers use herbaceous material and bulbs in several different ways. Evergreen herbaceous plants are excellent as ground cover under trees and shrubs. Some have eyecatching sculptural foliage like the tall *Phormiums*, and the spreading *Euphorbias* and *Bergenias*. In a mixed border, in conjunction with

Figure 12.1   The herbaceous border had its origin in the cottage garden.

Plate 8   Simple contrasts of foliage texture alone can be used to dramatic effect.

Plate 9   Grey foliage is a particularly successful foil for pink and mauve flowers.

Plate 10   A variety of bold foliage forms create a stimulating picture.

Plate 11 Laburnum avenues are an inventive use of flower form. The drooping flowerheads of wisteria can be used to similar effect.

Plate 12 Planting in the 'hot' yellow-red colour range warms a grey stone facade.

Plate 13   An inviting pedestrian route, enclosed by an avenue which offers protection, shelter and shade.

shrubs, trees and bulbs, herbaceous plants can give initial points of interest and colour until shrubs have matured. Conversely, shrubs can be used to form a permanent framework to contain the colourful, but ephemeral, deciduous perennials and bulbs.

The mixed border requires careful design to create a satisfactory 'structure' and to use the potential of seasonally changing colour masses effectively. Species with the best flowers often have poor foliage, and the flowers may only last a short time.

The scale of the design suggests the best approach to colour grouping. Scattered patches of colour may be suitable for a small-scale design where the viewer is in close contact but, on a larger scale, massed plants are more satisfactory as they avoid creating a spotty effect.

Herbaceous plants and bulbs can also be used informally in light woodland or wild gardens, where species are 'naturalized' — that is, grouped in drifts under trees or in rough grass. Given the right selection of species for the site, they can be self-perpetuating, requiring only a minimum of maintenance. If they are to store up sufficient food for the future in grassed areas, the grass around them must not be cut until the leaves of the bulbs have died down or the herbs set seed. The essential requirement is that they are located in places where long grass is acceptable in the design.

The generally softer colours of native bulbs and herbaceous plants, are to be preferred for naturalizing.

Figure 12.2   A plain hedge creates an effective backcloth for an herbaceous border.

Planting

A wide range of herbaceous plants can be sown from seed and many biennials and perennials are sold in containers. Some nurseries concentrate on providing plants for specific conditions, such as waterside or alpine gardens, and offer specialist technical advice.

It is unwise to make generalizations about the cultural requirements of herbaceous plants because the range is too broad. Some prefer a well-drained soil and sunny position; others prefer moist or shaded conditions. Thorough initial cultivation before planting is always essential and herbaceous planting benefits from the generous addition of organic matter to the soil. This cultivation should be done well in advance of planting, to allow for soil settlement, ideally in autumn so that the frost can then help to break up the heavier soils. Herbaceous plants should preferably be planted in the spring, from the end of February to early April.

Healthy bulbs should be firm and plump. Generally, they should be planted so that the top of the bulb is two or three times its diameter below soil level. Where a random effect is sought, the bulbs can be scattered over the ground, and planted where they fall.

Open, well-drained loam is preferable for most bulbs. To improve heavy, wet soils, a little sharp sand should be added at the base of the planting hole to reduce waterlogging. If the soil has been cultivated, it should be allowed to settle before planting.

Figure 12.3   Herbaceous plants in a light woodland where they are grouped in drifts under the trees or in rough grass.

Figure 12.4   *Above:* The textures of hard landscape and 'soft' herbaceous plants can be combined to pleasing effect.

Figure 12.5   *Right:* Herbaceous plants offer a fascinating variety of leaf textures.

CHAPTER 13

Design with Grasses

Grass is the most common ground cover in Britain and quickly becomes established, given good ground preparation. A broad range of grass species grow in this country, varying widely in colour, height, texture, growth rates and tolerances.

Most of the grasses used in landscape design have been bred from wild varieties to meet particular requirements, such as amenity use, sports activities, wet or shady situations or coastal sites. Grass is an ideal surface for walking on, except in very wet weather, as it is soft and regenerates easily after heavy wear, given correct care. It can be established by seeding or turfing.

Visually, grass is a restful evergreen carpet, that can be used to surface the 'floor' of the landscape. Where a design relies for its effect on subtly curved topography, evenly mown grass is an excellent finish. The fine, even texture and colour of well-maintained grass provides a sense of uniformity and spaceousnesss.

Interesting textural effects can be achieved by, say, mowing one area two or three times a season and an adjoining area more intensively, creating a contrast between a fine close-mown lawn and long grass with wild flowers.

In grass areas which are only cut once or twice a year, native wild flowers and bold swathes of bulbs can give extra interest from early spring to autumn. Careful timing of cutting is essential to ensure the continued survival of plants within the grass sward.

Several general points should be considered in the design of grassed areas. Their shape and size should take account of the type of mower to be used. Grass paths or swathes between planting areas must be wide enough to allow access for mowers without damaging plants or furniture. Trees and shrubs scattered within grass make mowing difficult and this invariably leads to bark damage at the base of the trunk. Grouping trees and shrubs together in large beds, with clean-cut curved edges, has the double advantage of stronger, simpler design and simplified mowing.

There are valuable economies to be made by concentrating grass in larger areas and eliminating narrow strips which are difficult to manage. Any width less than about 3.0m is more expensive to maintain per square metre, because a smaller hand-mower must be used. Further costs arise in maintaining a trimmed edge to paths or planting beds where grass is in small or narrow areas.

Because of root competition, tree shade and drip, it is difficult to establish and maintain grass satisfactorily below a dense canopy of trees. Shade-tolerant shrubs or herbaceous plants are at once more natural and more successful than grass under these conditions. If grass is to be established below trees, trees with a comparatively light canopy should be used, such as birch or false acacia, at widely spaced intervals.

The design of junctions between grass and other materials is important. It should be possible to mow right to the edge of a grassed area without damage either to mower or to neighbouring trees or shrubs, so grass should be 25–35mm above adjacent hard pavings and mowing margins and at least this amount above adjoining shrub beds.

A mowing margin is necessary against walls or fences, to offset the edge of the mown area at least 200mm. It can be constructed of brick, stone, concrete or gravel and should be set at least 150mm below the damp-proof course of buildings. Wider mowing margins, say 600mm or more, provide useful access for building maintenance, such as painting or window cleaning. If they are continued where there are planting beds, they also prevent soil being splashed onto the walls. However, gravel may scatter onto the grass and damage mower blades.

Careful route studies should precede the design of paths. Where potential footpath routes cross a grassed area, it is reasonable to expect people to take the shortest and most direct route. If it is difficult to anticipate 'desire lines' at the design stage, it may be sensible to allow them to become identified through the appearance of worn tracks before incurring the cost of hard pavings. A short paved section where wear is most intensive at the entrance and exit of a grassed space, or where footpaths converge, may be all that is needed.

Where pathways must be constructed at the outset, sharp corners and whimsical changes of direction should be avoided. Psychology can also play a part: most people prefer to walk along a valley rather than over a low mound. Where there are no distinct routes across a grassed area, hardwearing grass species can resist dispersed or random wear if watered during droughts.

Figure 13.1 Interesting textural effects can be achieved by contrasting grasses with different leaf and flower forms.

Seed Mixes

The seed mixture should be chosen to suit the site conditions and the function of the sward, as different activities have different requirements for colour, texture, ability to regenerate and maintenance. Bowling greens, for example, need a smooth velvety surface, while sports pitches require tough resilient grasses that are able to regenerate readily.

Special seed mixes are also available to suit particular site conditions, such as moderate shade under trees or for acid soils. The cost of grass-cutting in areas for general use can be reduced by the use of slow-growing 'low maintenance' grass varieties bred for their dwarf form.

Most mixtures contain several species to achieve an optimum performance. The major seed suppliers publish brochures on grass seed mixes and can supply mixes to meet special requirements (see Table 13.1).

Table 13.1   Range of seed mixes for various purposes

Light wear:	
Bowling greens	Chewings fescue and browntop bent
Fine lawns	Chewings fescue, browntop bent and slender creeping red fescue
Moderate wear:	
Residential areas	Perennial ryegrass, Chewings fescue, creeping red fescue, browntop bent and smooth-stalked meadow grass
Parks	
Heavy wear:	
Games pitches	Mostly perennial ryegrass, with some creeping red fescue and browntop
Low-maintenance mix suitable for sowing on poor soil and incorporating wild flower seeds	Chewings fescue, creeping red fescue, hard fescue, browntop bent and smooth-stalked meadow grass

Site Conditions

Mixes for general amenity use and sports turf require a well-drained soil which is reasonably fertile, with an open crumb structure. However, some grass species — such as fescues and bents — thrive on poor soils, where nutrient levels are relatively low, and can be sown directly onto suitable subsoil. The introduction of wild flowers into grassland is most successful on poorer soil with non-competitive grasses such as these.

As with other plants, grass must have air available to the roots, so a good soil structure must be retained throughout seed bed preparation. If the topsoil is compacted by heavy equipment, it must be restored to a good structure before seeding. Unnecessary compaction is a common problem on the majority of building developments and reflects a lack of awareness of the fact that the topsoil layer is a fragile material.

Good drainage is important, especially in areas of intense use on heavy soils. Subsoil drainage should be installed if there is any risk of standing water, to avoid deterioration of the sward. Finally, the detailed design must suit the specific site, soil and climatic conditions.

Expert advice should be sought about the construction of specialized facilities, such as playing fields, golf courses, and bowling greens.

Establishment

Whatever method of establishment is used, the soil preparation is of paramount importance, especially where intensive use is anticipated. A comparative summary of the advantages and disadvantages of seeding and turfing is shown in Table 13.2.

Ground preparation

Soil preparation, sowing or turfing should not be carried out when the soil is wet. After draining and subsoiling, if necessary, the topsoil on disturbed sites should be replaced to a depth of 150mm when the grass is to be used for amenity purposes. The topsoil must then be cultivated to a depth of 100mm, graded to final levels and recultivated to break it down into a fine tilth. Before sowing, all stones and debris over 25mm in any direction should be removed.

Table 13.2   Summary of the advantages and disadvantages of seeding and turfing

	Seeding	Turfing
Cost	Cheaper	3 to 5 times more expensive
Establishment	Takes 2–6 weeks to germinate, depending on temperature. Cannot be used for two to three months and requires a complete growing season before normal use and up to two season's growth for sports use.	Instant visual effect. Can withstand wear within two months or less.
Timing	Limited to the spring and autumn, avoiding periods of drought.	At any time, provided it can be watered, except when the soil is frostbound or waterlogged.
Quality	Seed mix can be exactly as specified to suit the site and purpose. Non-grass species can be included.	Turf of a consistent quality from a known seed mix is only available from a few sources. Unless strictly controlled at source, some turf may be weed-infested or uneven in thickness.
Supply	Can be conveniently stored until conditions are suitable for sowing.	Must be laid promptly, once lifted, to prevent drying out or rotting.
Suitability	Suitable for large sites and, if hydraulically applied, for steep and inaccessible areas.	Suitable for small areas. Can be established on steep banks, if pegged in place, but this is costly.

Sowing

The best time to sow depends on geographical location and soil type. Sowing may be carried out during April or preferably mid-August to mid-September, avoiding droughts. Because watering is expensive on large areas, it is normally limited to relatively small schemes or domestic gardens, where a uniformly good result is required.

During final cultivations, a pre-seeding fertilizer may be incorporated into the seed bed. Grass is broadcast by hand in very small areas, but the results tend to be uneven. The use of a seed distributor in two directions gives even coverage. Broadcast seed should then be rolled into the seed bed. For large areas, like sports fields, special grass seed drills that place the seed at the correct depth and press the seed bed together again by means of an integral roller are preferable to broadcasting due to better seed depth control, resulting in good germination. Mixtures of seeds in the drum of a broadcaster or drill must be continuously agitated, otherwise the smaller seeds settle out to the bottom.

Grass seed normally takes about two to three weeks to germinate. When it reaches 75mm high, stones should be picked out by hand and the grass rolled lightly on a dry day. A few days later, a light cut is used to remove the top 25mm. Light mowing should continue for the first few months until the roots have developed a good anchorage. Thereafter mowing should be done at the intervals required to maintain the grass within the intended height range.

Hydraulic seeding

This technique enables seeding to be carried out on steep banks, or even cliffs, over large areas of poor soils, subsoils and industrial spoil heaps, by means of special machines with a large tank and a pump able to pump slurries with up to 70 per cent solids. The slurry is sprayed from a high pressure gun or via extension hoses which can reach up to a distance of some 120–200 metres from the machine. Specifications vary considerably depending on the type of soil which is to be treated. Typically it would be a water-based mixture of wood pulp, peat, soil ameliorants together with grass seeds, fertilizers and a binder, which may be omitted where there is no risk of erosion.

The work is undertaken by specialist firms who can advise on specifications. Because of the relatively high cost of transporting and setting up the equipment, it is normally only used on larger schemes or where conventional sowing is impractical.

Turfing

Soil preparation for turfing is basically the same as for seeding, without the final cultivation to produce a fine tilth. Fertilizers and other soil ameliorants are incorporated into the topsoil, prior to laying.

Turf is generally supplied by specialist growers. Meadow turf is the most widely available and is the cheapest. Unfortunately, it is also likely to contain a high proportion of weeds and coarse grasses. A clear specification, coupled with careful inspection, is of particular importance if this cheap form of turf is used.

Sea-washed turf of fine leaved grasses, predominantly Fescues, from coastal areas used to be popular, but is comparatively expensive and disease-prone. It should be used only where conditions are similar to those where it was grown. Fine leaved grasses also occur in the downland turf to be found in southern England. These turves are of a better quality than meadow turf. The normal size of this type of turf is 300mm × 900mm × 25mm–35mm thick.

A number of turf suppliers provide a range of pre-seeded purpose grown turf for specialist applications such as cricket wickets, tennis courts, and bowling greens as well as for high quality amenity grass areas. Two types are generally available. Mature turf is harvested after up to about two years growth. The size of each turf is approximately 900mm × 2.100m. The other type is seedling turf which is harvested after some sixteen weeks growth. Seedling turves are larger measuring some 1m × 3m but they can be supplied smaller if required. These turves incorporate a fine mesh which increases their strength during lifting, handling and laying.

Proper handling of turf is important if it is to thrive. It should not be lifted in very wet or frosty weather and when brought on site it should be laid as soon as possible. Temporarily stored turf requires protection from drying winds and direct sunshine and should be stacked not more than four turves high. Turves which cannot be laid within three days should be spread out in a shady place and, in hot weather lightly watered.

The best time to carry out turfing is during the autumn or winter, provided that the soil is neither frozen nor waterlogged and the temperature is not falling. Turf laid in April may require regular watering in dry spells to prevent the turves shrinking and so opening up the joints.

Turves are laid with staggered joints and they should be gently pressed flat with a timber tamper. If necessary, they should be re-lifted and topsoil removed or added beneath them, until they are level. After laying, any gaps between the turves must be filled in with fine topsoil. The person laying turf or transporting it in a wheelbarrow should stand or kneel on a plank whilst working, to avoid deforming the surface.

On banks steeper than 1 in 2, turf should be laid horizontally or diagonally and held in place by wire or timber pins until it is well rooted. Seeded turves reinforced with plastic mesh are ideal for banks. Turf does sometimes slip, however, and planting shrubs or ground cover may well be a better long-term solution.

The edges of seeded areas should be defined by a line of turves to prevent loose topsoil spreading outwards and to ensure correct finished levels adjoining kerbs and pavings.

Maintenance

Proper ground preparation before seeding or turfing has already been emphasized. Adequate care during and after establishment is of equal importance.

Figure 13.2   Correct maintenance is essential for the successful establishment of wildflowers in grass.

Figure 13.3   A well maintained and healthy lawn provides a visually restfull evergreen carpet.

The height of cut should be 6mm for fine grass on bowling greens, about 25mm for general grassed areas, 20–50mm for football pitches throughout the year and 30–60mm for rugby pitches during the playing season. When cutting fine grass, the clippings are collected in the grass box and removed, but otherwise they are usually allowed to fly. Outfields, or semi-wild areas are normally only cut two or three times a year and if spring bulbs are present, are not cut until the bulb foliage has withered and died down. If the grass has been seeded with a wildflower mix or contains native summer flowers, it is cut in spring before the flower spikes have developed and again after they have set seed. Particular care is needed where there is a mixture of wild flowers with different flowering periods. When long grass is cut, the cuttings should be removed to prevent the swathes of rotting grass killing the grass beneath. In very dry summers, if there is a fire risk, additional cuts are necessary to keep the grass below about 30mm high.

Most lawn weeds can be controlled by frequent mowing. However, mowing too low, or scalping a lawn, or leaving the clippings on the surface, weakens the grass and encourages weeds, including mosses, to spread. Selective weedkillers should not be used until the sward is established, because they can damage young grass. Hand or chemical weeding of flat rosette perennial weeds, like dandelion, which escape mowing, is necessary.

Maintenance includes the application of compound fertilizers in spring, summer or autumn, in accordance with the maker's recommendations. Spring fertilizers have more nitrogen to encourage leafy growth and autumn fertilizers more phosphorous to promote root development. The overapplication of nitrogen in autumn encourages lush growth liable to frost damage and disease.

A newly established sward, if the soil is reasonably fertile, is likely to need only a light feeding at the end of the first summer. Minor depressions in the lawn can be filled by light top-dressing with sand and fine topsoil, or compost, early in the growing season.

CHAPTER 14

Plant Supply

Production of Plants

Many trees and shrubs are grown in nurseries in open ground for sale as bare-rooted stock. This is the most economic way of producing plants. They should be transplanted during the dormant period, generally between November and March, with care taken to prevent the roots from drying out, even for a short time, and to avoid physical damage at all stages, from lifting in the nursery to final planting.

Transplants are grown from seed, initially in sheltered seed beds, where they may spend one to two years. They are transplanted or undercut at least once in order to develop bushy root systems. During transplanting, poor stock is discarded. Transplants are available in a range of sizes from 300–1,200mm and are most commonly used for shelter belt or woodland planting.

A wide range of plants is now produced in containers allowing them to be transplanted at almost any time of year with comparatively little risk of damage, provided that the rootball remains intact. This method is essential for plants that do not tolerate root disturbance, such as hollies or junipers. Adequate watering is essential, if dry weather follows planting. Container-grown plants are more expensive than those grown in the open ground, because of the cost of labour and materials for potting-on into progressively larger containers to ensure good root development necessary for good establishment and stability. On the other hand, they have a high success rate and extend the planting season.

Source of Supply

The comparatively large numbers of plants used in landscape contracting work can be obtained from several sources:

1 Wholesale nurseries: stock large numbers of a fairly wide range of species, and are usually the cheapest source of plants. Many propagate their own plant material.
2 Retail nurseries: concentrate on offering an extensive range of popular species, holding only small numbers of each. They usually buy in their stock from wholesalers.
3 Forest nurseries: specialize in producing large quantities of forest transplants from seed, for forestry work or large-scale planting schemes.
4 Tree nurseries: specialize in the production of trees rather than other plant material. Trees are available from feathered to semi-mature trees and they may be open-ground or containerized. Some nurseries undertake the planting and aftercare of the trees they supply, which simplifies the question of liability should they fail to establish.

Transplanting client's trees

It is possible to transplant even relatively large trees which might otherwise be lost to development, but it is invariably much more expensive than planting nursery stock. To have a reasonable chance of survival, trees to be transplanted need to be prepared two years in advance, by root-pruning around a large rootball to encourage the growth of a mass of new fibrous feeding roots. This work is best undertaken by a specialist contractor. Good access for tree-lifting equipment is essential and the diameter of the tree's head must comply with Ministry of Transport's regulations if it is to be transported on public roads.

Site nurseries

On large-scale developments, it is sometimes practical and economic to set up temporary nurseries where small, cheap, plants are bought in bulk and 'grown on', so that they become acclimatized to the site conditions by the time they are planting size. Proper programming and professional management is essential to ensure good quality and timely production.

Nurseries vary considerably in the quality of plant material that they produce. In contract work, sources of supply are often nominated by the landscape architect to ensure that the plants supplied are of a consistent standard or to ensure that unusual plants can be individually selected at the nursery.

Size of Plant Material

Plants adapt to site conditions most readily if planted young. They suffer less root damage in planting, so establish themselves more quickly and grow faster than larger material, with fewer losses. However, their small size means that they have little initial visual impact.

Where a more immediate effect is required, and economy is not the overriding factor, it is, of course, possible to use larger plants, although the risks should be well understood. Larger trees often suffer a setback in growth for a number of years after planting.

Plant Names

Although plants are often referred to by their common or English name, one common name may cover many species or varieties of that plant – for example, oaks, maples, roses, irises. It is important, therefore, to use the full Latin name to ensure that the correct plants are supplied. The naming of wild plants is prescribed by the 'International Code of Botanical Nomenclature' whereas cultivated plants are covered by the 'International Code of Nomenclature for Cultivated Plants'.

Genera are shown with a capital initial letter – for example *'Acer'* (the maple family). Species are named with a small initial, for example:

Acer   platanoides
(genus)   (species)
(Common name: Norway maple)

Wild varieties and names of subspecies are written with a small initial letter, following the species to which they belong, for example:

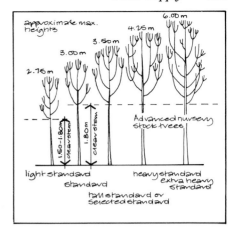

Figure 14.1   Tree sizes as described in BS 3639 : Part 1.

Acer   palmatum   coreanum
(genus)   (species)   (subspecies)
(Japanese maple with crimson autumn colour)

Cultivars are garden varieties and selected wild forms maintained in cultivation by vegetative propagation. Their names are written with a capital initial letter, in inverted commas, after the species to which they belong, for example:

Acer   platanoides   'Laciniatum'
(genus)   (species)   (cultivar)
(Common name: 'Eagle Claw Maple')

Hybrids are the result of crossing two species and are given a collective Latin name. Their hybrid origin is indicated by an '×' after the genus name, followed by the name of the hybrid with a small initial letter, for example,:

Acer × zoeschense

Specification

While the technique of landscape specifications lies outside the scope of this book, key criteria on plant quality include the following:

1   Plants must be true to name and to form, and be correctly labelled.
2   Plants should be selected, if possible, from suppliers whose material is grown under similar or *less* favourable conditions than those on the proposed site. Luxuriant plants produced in polythene tunnels have tender foliage and must be hardened off outdoors.
3   The size of plants should be carefully described, with reference to the appropriate part of British Standard – that is, 3936, 'Nursery Stock' or, for larger trees, BS 5236, 'Advanced Nursery Stock'. For container-grown plants, the size should be specified in litres – that is, in 1, 2, 3, 5, 8, 10, 12 or 16 litre pots. Because the quality of the root system is not necessarily in proportion to the soil volume, a few sample plants should be turned out of their pots, to inspect their roots. Designers who can inspect plants in the

nursery are in the strongest position to ensure that they get the best plant material.

Herbaceous plants should comply with BS 3936 : Part 10, 'Specification for ground cover plants' and the number of 'eyes' or growing points required should be stated for plants which will be dormant when purchased.

Bulbs should comply with BS 3936 : Part 9 'Bulbs, Corms and Tubers' and must be healthy and of sufficient size to flower in the season following planting.

4   Open-ground plants should have been transplanted or undercut during their period in the nursery. They should have a well developed root system to assist speedy establishment.

5   The roots of open-ground plants must not be exposed to drying winds, frost or become too hot at any time. They should not be allowed to dry out. Plants with polythene bags over the roots must not be left in the sun, because they soon overheat, damaging the plants.

6   Where rootballed plants are specified, the soil around the plant roots should be tightly wrapped with hessian or nylon netting so that the soil is not lost in transit.

7   Container-grown plants should be well established in their containers, but should not be 'pot-bound'.

8   Plants should be free from pests and diseases and not be in a damaged condition on receipt or at the time of planting.

9   Plants should be carefully handled to avoid shock or bruising. For instance, research has shown that throwing bundles of transplants to the ground from a lorry can considerably reduce their chances of survival.

10   Any minor damage during transit or planting, such as snapped small branches, should be cleanly trimmed back.

Figure 14.2   Container-grown plants which have become pot-bound should not be accepted.

Figure 14.3   A well organized shrub nursery with an overhead irrigation system.

11   On planting, shrub species which require annual pruning should be cut back, to encourage growth and bushiness.

12   At the completion of a contract, all listed plants should be checked to see that they are present, well established and in their correct positions.

CHAPTER 15

Planting and Establishment of Trees and Shrubs

Good ground preparation and planting techniques are essential for satisfactory growth, minimal losses, good establishment and ease of future maintenance.

The Planting Season

Deciduous trees and shrubs are planted during the dormant season, which is normally between November and March or April. Bare-rooted plants should only be lifted and planted during this period. Evergreens and conifers may be planted in late September or October or between March and early May. Herbaceous plants may be moved in September and October, or March and April. Container-grown material can be planted at any time of year except for periods of drought or frost.

Where possible, it is an advantage to plant deciduous trees and shrubs during the autumn to that they can settle in and make some root growth before spring. In reality, the time of planting within the dormant season is influenced by weather conditions and the effect they have on the delivery of plants from the nursery as well as the landscape contractor's work programme.

Planting Conditions

Planting must be delayed if the soil is wet, waterlogged or frozen, or if there are cold, drying winds. Fine roots dry out and die very rapidly in as little as a quarter of an hour in a strong wind. Bundles of bare-rooted plants should therefore be protected with moist peat under tarpaulins or in plastic perforated bags shaded from the sun until *immediately* before planting.

If bare-rooted plants arrive on site and planting has to be delayed, they must be heeled in for protection. One method is to prepare an open trench, with one side angled at 45°, for the plants to lie on. Bundles should be opened one at a time, to minimize the drying-out of the roots, and the plants laid out in line with the roots spread out. All the roots are then covered with fine soil and the topsoil is replaced to keep them moist.

Rootballed or container-grown plants can be left unplanted for several weeks, providing they are well protected from wind and frost and watered when necessary.

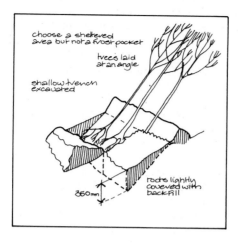

choose a sheltered
area but not a frost pocket

trees laid
at an angle

shallow trench
excavated

roots lightly
covered with
backfill

350mm

Figure 15.1   Heeling-in, temporary storage
of trees on site.

Tree Planting

The method of planting is determined by the size of the tree and the site
conditions. Traditional forestry techniques are often used for planting seedlings
or transplants in woodlands, shelter belts or hedgerows. Conversely, trees of
'standard' and 'advanced nursery stock' size require individual pits.

For large or difficult sites, an alternative to conventional methods is to sow
untreated tree and shrub seeds directly into the ground between November and
the end of December, and, where seed is pre-treated to stimulate it to break
dormancy, from January to March. Ground preparation and a clean seed bed
are of major importance. The seed is drilled, broadcast or spot planted according
to the size of seed, which varies greatly. After seeding, the area should be
mulched with chopped straw which should be 'tacked' with a bituminous
emulsion to hold it in place. A nurse crop, such as winter wheat or rye, or even
broom and lupins, is then used to act as a 'pioneer' giving shade and shelter to
young tree seedlings. Maintenance — selective weedkilling, for example —
depends on local circumstances but is generally quite low.

Planting preparation for traditional forestry techniques depends on the nature
of the proposed site. On undisturbed agricultural soils or old woodland sites,
planting may only require the removal of the surface vegetation with a sharp
spade - screefing. The simplest method with small trees is notch planting, where
a spade cut is made, the tree root slipped in, the spade withdrawn and the whole
sod firmly trodden down.

Where the soil is very wet or compacted, or the site is exposed, deep
ploughing with a powerful forestry plough is often necessary to improve
drainage for extensive woodland planting or afforestation. The furrow spacing
should correspond to the planting rows, and is usually at about 1.5m centres.
On wet soils, plants are placed into the well-drained soil near the top of these
ridges and, in dry or exposed situations, in the shelter of the ridge at the bottom
of the furrow. Where shelter or drainage is not a problem, planting is usually
halfway down the ridge.

Where soil conditions are adverse trees may be planted in pits and backfilled
with a mixture of topsoil and compost or fertiliser. In heavy clay soils there is a
danger that these pits may become waterlogged and land drainage is necessary.
Planting on low mounds can sometimes overcome this problem.

Pit-planting is the normal practice for all containerized nursery stock and for all trees larger than whips. The pits are dug to suit planting positions in advance of delivery, so that the trees are out of the ground for as short a time as possible. Before planting, the pit bottoms should be thoroughly broken up to a depth of 150mm and the sides loosened, particularly if formed with power augers or excavator buckets in clay soils, which can compress the sides until they are polished smooth.

Pits must be large enough in area to allow roots to be spread out in all directions without being cramped and should be at least 300mm deeper than the typical plant rootball, to allow the tree to be planted at its original depth. This level is usually visible as a ring-mark on the stem.

Where staking is required they should be driven firmly into the bottom of the pit before planting, on the windward side of the tree. The excavated topsoil should be thoroughly mixed with fertilizers and compost as required, to create a fine backfill which should be placed gently around the roots in layers, to ensure an even spread through the root system, and then well firmed in to eliminate air pockets. Trees should then be well watered in. Tree pits should be inspected subsequently for soil settlement and levels made up if necessary.

Tree Stability

Generally all trees over about 1.5m high require staking initially. The staking of smaller plants may be considered on exposed sites. Advanced nursery stock trees generally require two stakes. In fact the larger the tree, the longer it requires support before it can rely on its own root system. The best stakes are of peeled chestnut or larch because they decay slowly and are relatively cheap. Other timber should be treated with preservative against decay.

The traditional long stakes for larger trees are approximately 2.8m long, with a butt diameter of 75–100mm, driven 1.0m into the ground. They should be offset in position from the centre of the pit, on the windward side. The top of the stake for standard and advanced nursery stock trees should be set about 100mm below the level of the lowest branch.

Research by the Forestry Commission has shown that the use of shorter stakes has several advantages. They still protect tree roots from breakage when

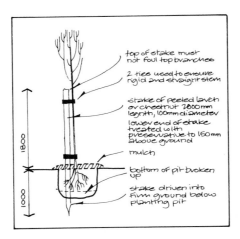

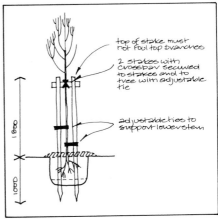

Figure 15.2   Standard tree with single long stake.

Figure 15.3   Two long stakes – used for larger trees, or on exposed sites.

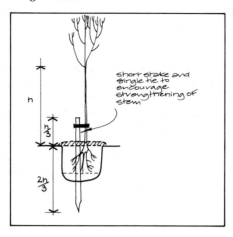

Figure 15.4   Standard tree with short stake.

the wind rocks the tree but, because the upper part of the stem is able to move with the wind, the development of supporting tissues in the trunk is also stimulated. They also give greater resistance to vandalism as the stem nearer the ground is less easily snapped off than where it is slender below the head.

Two tree ties are normally used to secure trees to the traditional long stakes but only one is required for shorter stakes. The top tie is fitted about 30mm below the top of the stake and the second about halfway down, or placed where a slightly bent stem might otherwise be bruised by contact with the stake. It is best to use one of the proprietary ties rather than cord. Ties should be inspected and adjusted as necessary shortly after planting and annually thereafter to take account of the growth in the tree's girth.

Wire guying, secured above or below ground is an alternative means of supporting larger trees. Semi-mature trees can be anchored with underground guys, strapped over their rootball and fixed to sleepers below ground.

Transplanting semi-mature trees is an operation which should be undertaken only by specialist contractors and liability for replacement, extending to three or five years, is an essential feature of the contract. Semi-mature trees should be obtained from reputable firms some of whom will undertake to supply, plant and provide maintenance for the period of the guarantee. For further details, see BS 4043, 'Recommendations for transplanting Semi-Mature trees', which covers all aspects of this operation from the selection of the trees to their after-care.

Shrub Planting

Shrub beds should have a minimum topsoil depth of 300mm and preferably 450mm. Before placing the topsoil, the subsoil should be well-broken up to a depth of at least 150mm to facilitate drainage. A hole should be dug for each shrub, large enough to accommodate the roots without bending them, any roots that have begun to grow spirally in a container should be eased outwards. The shrub should be held so that the soil mark on the stem is at the new ground level whilst the hole is backfilled with fine topsoil mixed with any necessary fertilizers. After planting, the soil around the plant must be firmed by treading and the plant well watered.

Rootballed and pot-grown plants should be watered thoroughly before planting. When placed in their pits, any hessian coverings should be loosened but not necessarily removed as they rot away in due course. Plastic netting or polythene containers should be carefully removed before planting.

Mulching

Mulching is beneficial to trees and shrubs. A loose layer, generally 50–75mm deep, of organic or inorganic material is spread over the bare ground after planting. A good organic mulch retains moisture, restricts weed growth and, when it decomposes, adds nutrients to the soil. The soil must be thoroughly cleaned of weeds before mulching. Mulch is best applied while the ground is damp.

Without a mulch soil has to be kept weed-free by hand-weeding or by the use of herbicides. Hand-weeding, including hoeing, is an expensive, labour-intensive operation. On the other hand, herbicides may adversely affect some young shrubs, and most herbaceous plants are susceptible. Furthermore, after applying herbicides, it is also still necessary to work through planting beds by hand, to remove the dead weeds.

Suitable materials for organic mulches include coarse or pulverized bark, moist peat, well rotted farmyard manure or spent mushroom compost. Bark is effective as a weed suppressor, if it is spread 50–75mm deep. The finer grades of bark create an attractive finish but a coarser grade should be used where windblow or water run-off is anticipated. In areas where vandalism is prevalent, some forms of bark mulch may present a fire risk. Bark mulches last about three years. During the process of decomposition, nitrogen is lost from the soil, so nitrogenous fertilizer should be added to compensate for the loss.

Peat, manure and mushroom compost, whilst providing some useful nutrients, also form a seed bed for young weeds and the use of herbicides may still be necessary.

Inorganic mulches can include naturally occurring materials such as washed gravels or pebbles or synthetic sheet materials like black polythene film. Gravel or pebbles are relatively cheap, have an attractive finish and are quite successful in suppressing weeds. Their use is generally confined to small areas such as courtyards where they can be an important visual aspect of the design. Sheet materials, including porous synthetic membranes, can be very effective in retaining moisture in the soil and suppressing weeds but, uncovered, are unattractive and so are most commonly used below other mulches such as bark or pebbles.

Individual trees may be mulched with organic or inorganic material. In paved areas when tree grilles are used, the trees may be mulched with pea shingle below the grill. In rural situations synthetic membranes can be cut to form tree 'spats' to suppress weed competition at the base of young trees but, although effective, this is an unsightly method of mulching and other materials should be used in visually prominent locations.

Protection of Plants

In urban areas, plants are vulnerable to damage by vehicles and by vandalism. In the country most damage is caused by animals.

The type of tree protection should be related to the overall design. In a formal setting an expensive circular cage of metal palings may be appropriate. Along urban roads and in car parks, stout timber bollards, about a metre away from the tree trunk, may suffice. Shrub planting in or around car parks can be protected from vehicles by low timber or metal rails or at much greater cost by placing the shrubs in raised planters. A strip of paving or gravel, about 600mm wide, *behind* the kerbs allows vehicles to oversail without damaging shrubs. Where narrow planting beds are likely to be trampled over, a single wire 600mm high, stretched though the planting may be sufficiently discouraging. A temporary fence such as chestnut paling is usually necessary to discourage casual trampling through larger areas until the planting becomes established.

Protection against vandalism is not easily achieved. It is a far-reaching problem which can only be resolved by thoughtful design. For example, standard trees should be placed in a thicket of tough and spiny shrubs, rather than in open grass areas. If trees are to be planted where they cannot easily be protected – for example, close to a footpath – advanced nursery stock or semi-mature trees should generally be selected.

In rural areas, the method of protecting young plants from damage by animals depends on the extent of the planted area and the animals concerned. Individual trees can be protected from small animals by tree guards. Spiral plastic guards protect against rabbits and the small 'clip-on' tube guards also offer some protection against voles, but these smaller guards can be rendered ineffective after heavy snow which raises the surrounding levels. The taller, staked, tree tubes are particularly valuable where deer are a problem. The wind shelter that they provide can also enhance the growth rate of some species. Where only a small number of trees are being planted, tree guards can also be made on-site from plastic mesh or galvanized rabbit wire.

Individual trees in parkland are best protected from grazing animals by a timber post and rail fence enclosure, some two metres away from the stem.

For protection of larger plantations, an enclosing fence may be more cost-effective than individual guards. Protection against stock requires a sturdy strained wire fence, 1.2m high, with the top strand barbed. Deer can only be kept out by a wire mesh deer fence, 1.8m high. Strained wire and post and rail fencing can be rabbit-proofed by the addition of wire mesh, the lower 150mm of which is turned outwards and buried. See Vol. 2 chapter 13, page 111.

Protection from Grass Cutting

Mowers and strimmers damage the base of young trees in grass if the machinery comes into contact with the bark. To avoid this, a metre diameter circle of bare,

Figure 15.5   Stone setts make an effective mowing edge between a lawn and shrub beds.

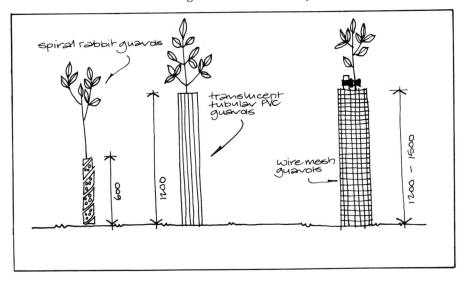

Figure 15.6   Types of guards to protect young trees from grazing animals.

weed-free soil around the trunk should be maintained. In plantations, securely fixed tree tubes provide some protection from strimmers used to keep competing vegetation in check.

Maintenance

All plants compete for space, light and nutrients. Weeding is an essential maintenance operation, to ensure good establishment by reducing competition. Research by the Forestry Commission indicates that a one metre radius weed-free circle around feathered or standard trees is the minimum to achieve good growth rates. Of all the weeds, grasses are the most competitive, particularly when cut, as that stimulates regrowth and encourages them to take up water and nutrients otherwise available to the tree. In most situations, trees planted amongst shrubs establish more successfully than those in grass, because they suffer less from competition.

After hard frosts and severe storms, when the soil around root systems is loosened, all newly planted shrubs and trees require firming in.

Regular watering in dry spells is only necessary where the soil moisture levels have fallen too low. If watering is necessary, it is more effective to soak the soil thoroughly to a good depth occasionally than to sprinkle it frequently. Watering is especially important in dry, urban situations where much of the precipitation is drained into storm water drains from paving.

It is good management practice, at the end of each growing season, to note any dead or failing plants, so that they can be replaced during the following planting season. In forestry, this replacement is known as 'beating up'.

An annual inspection should be made to adjust tree stakes and ties and to carry out any necessary pruning. In the longer term, trees in plantations must be thinned at appropriate stages in their development. Stakes should be removed from standard trees as soon as the natural root anchorage has developed. All temporary protective fencing should be removed as soon as all the plants, or trees, are reasonably well established and trampling is no longer likely.

CHAPTER 16

Woodlands

After the last Ice Age, about 12,000 years ago, the British Isles became almost completely covered with forest. From the Neolithic period onwards, extensive clearings were made for agriculture as the human population expanded, until about 1100AD, when the rate of clearance slowed considerably. From the twelfth century onwards, very little change occurred in the extent of Britain's woodland cover until the First World War.

Today, only a few small, scattered remnants of woodland remain which are thought to have an undisturbed historical continuity with the original 'wildwood', such as parts of Wistmans' Wood on Dartmoor. Almost all of the sites which have always been wooded have been replanted, managed or otherwise affected by man at some time. The remainder have been planted or have arisen by natural recolonization of disused agricultural or industrial land.

Commercial Forestry

Until recently, the pressure to maximize agricultural production made most lowland areas of Britain unavailable for forestry. However, on the less fertile soils that cover much of the uplands, commercial forestry can be the most economically viable land use, because the mild, wet British climate encourages some of the fastest timber growth in northern Europe. Broadleaved trees grown in this situation have a minimal value as firewood and the only conifers native to the British Isles are the Scots pine, juniper and yew, so the majority of our productive forests are of introduced coniferous species. Broadleaves are less attractive commercially because they take longer than softwoods to reach a marketable size — 70 to 100 years rather than 50 to 60 years.

In modern upland conifer forests, a fairly restricted range of species is planted because of the harsh climate and poor soil conditions. The predominant trees are evergreen conifers — spruce, fir, and pine — with the deciduous larch and broadleaves providing visual and habitat diversity. Open space is also planned in the forest as rides, roads, streamsides, and deer glades. Trees are often planted as substantial areas of single species, although mixtures are used in some areas. This is partly for silvicultural and economic reasons but also to achieve the appropriate scale of forest in the landscape.

In order to secure a supply of home-produced timber, following the massive depletions of the First World War, as much land as possible was planted as quickly as possible by the newly formed Forestry Commission. This led to the details of the landform, vegetation patterns, outcrops of rocks and streams being hidden beneath the forest canopy. Forest outlines often followed the rectilinear enclosure and ownership boundaries. This lack of response to the

Figure 16.1 Early conifer plantations attracted criticism because they were often rectilinear in outline and obliterated details of the landscape.

Figure 16.2 Small deciduous woodlands are still valued for game coverts, shelter and firewood, as well as for amenity.

landscape was recognized quite early on and led to the appointment of a landscape consultant to look at the problem in the early 1960s.

Sylvia Crowe's pioneering forest design work for the Forestry Commission in the 1960s and 1970s has led to much greater sensitivity to local landscape character in forestry design. Many of the Commission's forests which are now in their second rotation have been greatly improved during the felling and replanting cycle.

Broadleaved Woods

Numerous small, mainly broadleaved, woodlands, rather than extensive tracts of forest, tend to be features of the lowland agricultural landscape of Britain.

Before the eighteenth century, rural settlements were self-sufficient in timber production, with small woods and copses planted and managed for the needs of the immediate community. Traditionally, deciduous trees were planted (or, if self-sown, were allowed to remain), on farms to give shelter for crops and stock, for conversion to timber and firewood, for game coverts and for amenity. All of these objectives are still valid today but, until quite recently, the high value of agricultural land and the impact of EEC Common Agricultural Policy intervention on British farming reduced the incentive to retain woods, farm coppices or even hedges. Farmers were reluctant to spend time thinning, fencing or weeding the small areas of coppiced and mixed woods that were once a feature of every farm and, as they deteriorated, the land was frequently converted to agricultural use. As a result, it is said, British farmers have largely lost their woodland skills during the past 40 years' agricultural intensification.

Integrated farming and forestry is a more traditional pattern of woodland management in Europe, especially for example, in Norway and France, where, particularly in less productive areas, farmers have retained many more of their traditional woodland management practices.

Dutch Elm disease, and major changes in agricultural practice, have led to the removal of thousands of miles of hedges and their associated trees, which has denuded the lowland farmed landscape of much of its tree cover in the second half of the twentieth century.

Under the present re-evaluation of farm surplus, all kinds of woodland and commercial forestry are likely to become increasingly popular. Existing small woods are again being managed for a range of objectives: timber production, game coverts, nature conservation, wind shelter or landscape features. Landowners are now being encouraged to plant new broadleaved woods in the lowlands through the Woodland Grant Scheme or Farm Woodland Scheme. Many of the design principles which have been evolved by the Forestry Commission are being applied to the planning of these new small woods.

Design of New Woodlands

The first step in the design of a plantation is a visit to the key viewpoints from which it will be seen, in order to make a broad analysis of the existing landscape and to take panoramic photographs. Alternative proposals can be drawn on to transparent overlays placed over the photographs for evaluation. The preferred scheme is then accurately plotted onto an Ordnance Survey map (preferably 1:10,000 scale).

A study of the landscape into which the plantation must fit should enable one to assess whether the scene is dominated by the landform or by the pattern of existing trees and hedgerows. If there is doubt about this, the influence of the

Figure 16.3   Thoughtful forestry design can enhance the landscape.

landform should predominate.

Having analysed the setting, three main aspects of the plantation design are considered: its scale, shape and diversity.

The scale of each forest block should relate to the size of the open spaces in the landscape and the amount of woodland which will be visible from specific viewpoints. On sweeping open hillsides, small plantations can look out of place. Their apparent area can be maximized by planning elongated shapes and by overlapping several small blocks. By contrast, woodlands in an area of hedged fields should be in keeping with the scale of the local enclosures, unless they follow a strong topographical feature such as a steep river valley.

The plan shape of plantations is particularly important in hilly areas where the edge should be irregular, in a manner that reflects the landform, for example, angular in the craggy Lake District or smoothly curved in the rolling hills of the Borders. Edges should generally rise in hollows and fall around spurs, emphasizing the flow of the landform, and on open hillsides the outside edge of a plantation should taper diagonally to the lower edge. Unnatural plan forms such as those with right angles, parallel edges, long straight edges and edges running perpendicular to or following the contours, should be avoided. In the past, rectilinear plantations have been created by planting right up to ownership boundaries, which seldom follow curving lines or natural features. By leaving some land unplanted within the acquistion boundary, more sympathetic shapes can be created. In lowland areas, more geometric shapes with straight edges may be appropriate, so long as they fit into the existing field boundary patterns.

The shape of internal edges should also be considered at this stage, avoiding

Figure 16.4 Diversity can be introduced by enriching existing features, such as streamsides, with native broadleaved trees and shrubs.

the traditional grid-iron patterns for rides or compartments. Boundaries, fire breaks and roads should relate to the underlying landform and topographical features.

Diversity may be introduced in a number of ways, but the scale should again relate to the landform or to the existing vegetation structure. The measures which create visual interest tend also to promote a richer ecological diversity (see 'Conservation' p.119). Diversity needs to be considered in a forward-looking way as the patterns of initial planting determine the future appearance of woodland through the processes of felling and re-stocking. The treatment of forestry margins is particularly important. The vertical 'wall' of a conifer plantation can be softened by irregular groups of broadleaved trees along the edge which are most effective if they also penetrate into the conifer stand. The edges of broadleaved woods may be similarly uneven, and in both cases, the appearance and ecological diversity can be enhanced by the introduction of native shrubs and infrequently mown grass. Within the plantation, visual interest and variety of habitat are provided if craggy outcrops, stream or lake margins and existing areas of scrub, trees or hedges are left unplanted. Clumps of broadleaved trees and native shrubs may also be effectively grouped around such features.

A diversity of tree species within a broadleaved plantation is visually desirable, but the proportions of deciduous and evergreen species in mixtures have to be carefully handled. Small clumps of broadleaved trees scattered through a conifer stand can produce an unsatisfactory "spotty" effect. Both geometrically arranged mixtures and angular stands of larch contrasting with neighbouring evergreen compartments appear harshly incongruous in winter. The most visually disturbing combination is the striped pattern created where conifers are planted as a "nurse" crop to shelter slower growing hardwoods; for instance, three rows of spruce and then one of oak. The conifers are then harvested at a relatively early age, for pit props and pulp-making, leaving space for the hardwoods to develop for sawn timber. From a landscape point of view, this system is best avoided except in level lowland areas where the pattern cannot be perceived from the ground.

A few key points should be borne in mind when planning the introduction of broadleaved trees into conifer plantations. Local species should be used, that will thrive on the site, and horticultural varieties should be avoided. The broadleaved trees should be planted in clumps and irregular shapes, located where they emphasize or enhance the landform — to highlight valleys or soften skylines, for example — or relate to existing hedges or scrub.

Despite the volume of criticism of our commercial forests, when the time comes to harvest the timber, the impact of clear felling often provokes a good deal of public outcry. Felling areas, or "coupes" can diversify the scene, but

Figure 16.5   Selective felling ensures continuity of habitat and minimizes visual disruption.

again their size must be in scale with the landscape. The potential damage of windthrow may determine the shape of felling coupes, but taking a calculated risk is to be preferred to creating or maintaining intrusive windfirm edges. Felling on skylines should be planned to avoid both slivers of open land above afforested slopes and the "castellated" silhouette which can result from small coupes or selective felling.

Selective felling is an alternative method of harvesting mixed-age stands of woodland. Only the more mature trees are removed, leaving the younger or slower-growing trees to develop, so that the ground is never completely cleared. This method is more costly in management and labour and is only really viable in the lowlands or in very stable stands in the uplands, because exposure to high winds makes the remaining trees vulnerable to windthrow. Selective felling is more time consuming and more expensive than clear felling, because of the difficulties of felling and extraction without damaging other trees. Nevertheless, taking a long-term view, this traditional method of harvesting timber is undoubtedly the best way to conserve the ecosystem, the topsoil and the visual continuity of the landscape.

Conservation

Unless a wood contains particular rarities, its conservation value is usually assessed in terms of the number of different plant and animal species present. This can be maximized by providing as wide a variety of habitats as possible, but continuity of these habitats is also vital, to maintain viable populations.

Continuity is important both in space and time. Spatially inter-connected areas of a particular habitat form a far more valuable territorial range for animals (to feed or breed) and for plant dispersal than isolated pockets. Such networks can be provided in tandem with good visual design, e.g. by linking broadleaved trees, scrub and open ground along streamsides, roads and rides with similar vegetation outside the wood.

The cycle of tree growth in timber plantations and coppiced woods creates an ever-changing environment, open and light in the early years and increasingly shaded as the tree canopies close together overhead. Few species of associated plants and animals thrive at all the stages of the trees' growth so, if an extensive area of woodland is at a uniform stage in the cycle, this limits its conservation value. In a timber plantation on a long rotation, some plant and animal populations may not survive from one early, open, well-lit stage to the next and so may be lost from the area altogether. Thus the conservation value of woodlands can be greatly increased by managing the tree crop as a mosaic of different aged stands thereby providing continuity through time of the different woodland habitats. The visual effects of such a patchwork require careful handling, as described under woodland design.

The dense shade cast by some conifer plantations makes their cyclical effect on the ground flora particularly extreme, shading it out altogether at an early stage. Early and heavy thinning can help to maintain at least some other plants beneath for a longer period.

It is not only the effects of changing light conditions that affect dependent wildlife. Alterations in the physical structure of a wood affect the number of birds present, this being at a maximum when the vegetation layers are most diverse. Half-grown coppice thicket with standard trees seems to provide optimum conditions for birdlife.

Management of woodland margins to provide continuity of habitat plays an

Figure 16.6   Mixed broadleaved woodlands allow light through their canopies, which permits the co-existence of a richly varied ground flora.

important role in conservation. If irregular clumps of native shrubs are planted, or are allowed to colonize the edge, they provide a wide variety of food and habitat, particularly if they are cut back every few years to maintain low scrub. The value of undisturbed grassland habitat alongside rides can be increased by cutting each side in alternate years to provide continuity of herbaceous seed sources.

Mixed broadleaved woodland has a higher conservation value in lowland Britain than evergreen conifer stands, for several reasons. By allowing light through their canopies in springtime, deciduous trees permit the coexistence of spring-flowering ground vegetation, such as bluebells and primroses, even when they are mature. The leaf litter breaks down to a neutral humus more quickly than conifer needles which tend to create acid ground conditions. Native broadleaved trees also support many more specifically dependent insects, fungi, and other wildlife than introduced trees. Broadleaved woods often contain a greater variety and higher number of birds than conifer stands. There are a few birds which are almost absent from conifer woods, such as the nuthatch, nightingale and marsh tit and, equally, there are also those found only in association with conifers, such as the crossbill, firecrest, siskin and crested tit. Birdlife can therefore be richest in woods which are a mixture of broadleaf and conifer.

When trees are being harvested, the impact on wildlife should be minimized by felling in winter rather than in spring when birds are nesting and the ground vegetation is in flower. Physical damage to the ground, leading to erosion and waterlogging, should be avoided. Streambanks are especially fragile. After felling, varieties of habitat can be maintained by leaving some branchwood strewn on the woodland floor and a few standing dead trees for nest-holes and insects. The retention of some good specimens, or clumps, of thriving trees, and between 20–40 standard trees per hectare in coppice, is also very beneficial.

Finally, an important conservation issue when planning woodlands is where not to plant. In the lowlands, new woods should only be planted into arable or rotational pasture land. It is important that old undisturbed grasslands are not included, since these tend to be a rare habitat. Existing hedges and trees and any undisturbed vegetation around them should also be retained within new woods, to provide a source of colonizing plants and insects.

Any sites within a proposed plantation identified as having particular conservation value should be left unplanted, together with a surrounding buffer area at least as wide as the anticipated tree height. Open land linking them up with similar habitats should also be retained if possible. Planting around such sites should be sympatheticaly designed to avoid compromising their ecological value.

Archeological conservation is also carried out at the planning stage. The county or regional archaeologist may be consulted to check whether there are any sites of interest on the land concerned. These should be left unplanted, with their boundaries designed to avoid a geometric shape.

Recreation and Forestry

Changing patterns of work and leisure have resulted in an increase in recreation pressure on all accessible woodland. The Forestry Commission has permitted pedestrian access to all of its forests, except where this is precluded by conservation priorities or where land is leased and the conditions of the lease preclude it. Visitors are positively encouraged to many of the Commission's forests, especially the 'Forest Parks'. Walking, riding, picnicking, fishing, orienteering, camping and caravanning are some of the many activities catered for. Walks are often combined with nature trails, making use of existing fire breaks, rides and extraction routes.

The passive pleasure that many people find by merely looking at a richly varied wood, or simply enjoying the quiet lofty spaces within, surrounded by unfamiliar bird calls and scents, is probably of even more popular significance than the more easily defined sporting activities. Good design can enhance visitors' pleasure in the forest, by opening up or framing special views, giving access to places of special interest and creating a variety of habitats.

With skilled management, the multiple use of the land can be sustained with little loss of productivity even with high numbers of visitors. To avoid disturbance to wildlife — for instance, during the breeding season — vulnerable sites can be protected by channelling the public into less sensitive areas.

Urban Woodlands

The smallest areas of woodland can be important assets in an urban environment, not only for visual relief, but also for recreation, wildlife conservation and education. In urban planning, a network of woodland can contribute far more to landscape quality than disconnected patches of tree planting by providing corridors for recreation and wildlife. Woodland can also form an excellent buffer between densely populated areas and agricultural land. Indeed, woodland planting on derelict land in urban areas is now being actively promoted. This often requires special treatment to deal with difficult ground conditions and even toxicity.

It is important to assess the attitude of the local community to urban woodland early in the planning stage, as the support and cooperation of local communities are always vital to the success of any urban woodland projects. People vary widely in their attitude towards the presence of forest trees in towns and cities. Many value existing woods, but others feel that woods are a place of potential danger. Open land between woodland and homes can diminish the perceived threat to people living nearby and also avoids overshadowing in winter.

Clearly, the management of woodland where provisions for public access is the highest priority differs from that for timber production or for wildlife conservation. In the Netherlands, Belgium and West Germany, as well as in the British New Towns, there is now a considerable body of experience in the establishment and management of urban woodlands. This has led to the development of techniques to deal with the damage inflicted to woodlands by intensive human use.

Ideally, woodland planting should be carried out in advance of building development and enclosed with protective fencing before any construction begins. In established urban woodland, essential management tasks include thinning of excessive undergrowth and the removal of diseased or over-mature trees. Both of these would be retained for their habitat value in rural woods where public safety is not paramount.

Where replanting is carried out, the young trees will require protection until they have become established. It may also be necessary to provide protective fences around areas of the wood on a rotation basis, to allow for the regeneration of the ground flora. Some local land drainage may be necessary, as well as the regular maintenance of footpaths and bridleways, to allow people to walk through the wood dryshod.

Ancient Woodlands

Ancient woodlands occupy a unique and irreplaceable position in the history of nature and man, and are the richest terrestrial ecosystems in Britain.

The term 'ancient' is usually applied to woodlands known to have existed before 1700AD, whilst those planted after that date are known as 'recent'. Some ancient woodlands began to develop from about the time of the last Ice Age.

Most of these very old woodlands are 'semi-natural', since they have at some time been affected by the activities of man. Woodlands which have never been clear-felled are termed 'primary', and 'secondary' woods are those that have reappeared on land once cleared for farming. The former are extremely rare and are found in very inaccessible areas which are too steep or too wet to farm.

There were few detailed maps or surveys published before 1600, so the initial recognition of a possible ancient woodland usually has to be made on the basis of field evidence. Certain tree and herb species can provide clues to the antiquity of woodland, but the same species do not necessarily indicate ancient origins in all parts of the country. The presence of, for example, wych elm *(Ulmus glabra),* small-leaved lime *(Tilia cordata)* or field maple *(Acer campestre)* may indicate considerable age, as may dog's mercury *(Mercurialis perennis)* or Solomon's seal *(Polygonatum multiflorum).* The presence of earthworks, banks with ditches and old tracks may also indicate ancient woodland locations.

There are two distinct traditional woodland management systems: coppice and wood pasture. In coppiced woods, the 'underwood' trees are cut down to within 100–200mm of the ground every 7–25 years, depending on the species. The cut wood is used for fuel, poles and woodcrafts. The most common underwood species are hazel, sweet chestnut, hornbeam and alder. To supply sawn timber as well, scattered trees of, for example, oak or ash are allowed to grow to maturity – a system known as 'coppice with standards'.

Woodlands managed on a coppice rotation are of considerable ecological value, arising from the ever-changing mosaic of tree ages, which provides varying vegetation structure and light conditions, with a corresponding diversity of habitats for a wide range of insects, birds and small mammals.

The decline of traditional woodland management, especially of coppiced woods, through falling demand for woodland products, has accelerated during the last 30 years. Now, due to agricultural land 'set-aside' and the popularity of wood-burning stoves, there may be a return to labour-intensive coppice woodland.

Wood pasture developed in times when grazing was allowed in woodlands and is rarely practised now. The wood consists of clear-stemmed trees, with the herb and shrub layer reduced to a few grazing-tolerant species. Parkland can be considered to be an extreme form of wood pasture, where single trees, with their lower canopy cropped level to the height to which cattle or deer can stretch, are scattered through grassland.

Figure 16.7 Woodlands managed as coppice with standards are of considerable ecological value. Figure 16.10 illustrates a similar hazel wood after coppicing.

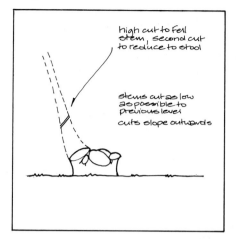

high cut to fell
stem, second cut
to reduce to stool

stems cut as low
as possible to
previous level

cuts slope outwards

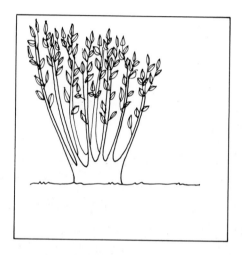

Figure 16.8 *Above left:* The start of the coppice cycle. The correct method of cutting a coppiced plant back to the stool.

Figure 16.9 *Above right:* During the next summer, new shoots arise from the stool.

Figure 16.10 *Left:* After several seasons regrowth, a dense thicket can develop.

Wood pasture or parklands do not support the same abundance of species as coppice, but they are valuable as a home to a different selection of wildlife. In them can be found broad-spreading individual trees of great age, which support a wide range of lichens and insects.

Since the 1950s many valuable ancient woodlands have been cleared for agriculture or development, or converted to conifer plantations. No amount of replanting can replace the complexity of a woodland ecosystem built up over the centuries, so there are strong reasons for identifying, retaining and providing suitable management for remaining ancient woodlands.

In summary, the most important points to consider when managing ancient woodland are:

1 Use of traditional management techniques.
2 Avoidance of clear felling.
3 Retention of the diversity of the woodland structure and flora by retaining areas of coppice, scrub and open glades. Wet areas, streams and ponds should be retained for the further diversity they contribute.
4 Use of native species, grown from local seed sources, when replanting, but making use of natural regeneration wherever possible. There are often many

saplings that can be selectively managed in these woods. By excluding grazing animals, scrub regenerates naturally into woodland with little additional cost.

5   Retention of ancient trees that form invaluable habitats for insects and birds, despite their poor timber value, and of dead wood which supports a unique range of fungi and insects.

6   Protection of all archaelogical features such as banks, ditches, ridge and furrow fields, earthworks, old lanes and ruins.

7   The use of accurate ecological surveys, to guide management operations.

Advice on ancient woodlands is available to landowners or to the public from most county councils, local naturalists' trusts, the Nature Conservancy Council and the Forestry Commission.

Figure 16.11 A recently coppiced hazel wood, with some of the small roundwood harvested from it in the foreground. Note the oak standard in the background.

Glossary

The * denotes definitions based on British Standards see p.130.

Advanced nursery stock*	Deciduous trees between 3.6–6.0m high and 12–20cm girth or conifers between 2.0–3.5m high, which have been transplanted a number of times and root-pruned to prepare them for transplanting to their final site at an advanced stage of growth.
Amenity woodland	Woodland planted or managed mainly for visual, shelter and game conservancy reasons rather than timber production.
Annual*	A plant which germinates, flowers, fruits and dies within a year.
Arboriculture	The cultivation and care of trees.
Bare-rooted plant*	A plant grown in the open ground and lifted without soil around its roots, for replanting elsewhere.
Biennial*	A plant which grows from seed one year and flowers, fruits and dies the next.
Broadleaved tree	A tree with broad flat leaves belonging to the group of plants known as *Dicotyledons*, characterized by leaf veins arranged in a branching (not parallel) pattern. The branching configuration of broadleaved trees is also random in pattern.
Bulb*	In horticulture, the term 'bulb' is used for plants which produce their leaves and flowers directly from an underground storage organ. Botanically, the term 'bulb' is applied to an underground modified stem bearing a number of swollen fleshy leaf bases or scale leaves in which food is stored, the whole enclosing the next year's bud.
Clear felling	Felling of all trees within a particular area of woodland.
Climax vegetation	The climax or end-point of a colonizing succession of plant communities. The ecological climax is a mature, relatively stable area of vegetation, the species composition of which will not change unless the prevailing conditions alter.
Community	A group of plants and/or animals which are often found to live together in the same habitat. The grouping can be described by the presence of one or more characteristic species.
Compaction (of soil)	Destruction of soil structure by pressure of heavy machinery or prolonged foot-traffic. This results in destruction of soil fauna and changes in soil bacteria from aerobic to anaerobic.

Competition	Occurs when plants compete with each other for the available light, water and nutrients.
Conifers*	Trees which bear cones. The term also applies to yew, juniper and Maidenhair tree *(Ginkgo biloba)* in which the cone is modified. Conifer leaves are usually needle-like or scale-like, with parallel veins, and most conifers are evergreen.
Conservation	In this context, the management of an area of vegetation in its present state and, ideally, optimization of its potential by active measures, including restoration, maintenance of the physical environment and replanting. 'Preservation' in the sense of maintaining a static situation is not possible with a living ecosystem.
Container-grown plants*	Plants grown in containers other than clay pots.
Coppice	Woodland managed by cutting trees down to ground level on a 7–20 year rotation. Regrowth of several buds around the stump (or 'stool') produces reasonably straight young poles, used for firewood, pulp, or 'roundwood' craft products (see Chapter 16).
Corm*	A bulb-like, but solid modified, underground stem, each new corm being formed at the top of that of the previous year.
Crown*	The base of an herbaceous perennial, where stem and root meet and from which fresh shoots and roots arise.
Cultivar	A garden variety of a form found in the wild, which does not breed true from seed and is maintained in cultivation by vegetative propagation.
Deciduous*	A plant that sheds all its leaves before the emergence of next season's leaves. Beech and hornbeam often retain dead leaves however.
Desire lines	Direct routes which people want to follow.
Dominant species	The species in a plant community which, by its size or abundance, determines the characteristics of that community, such as the beech tree in beech woodland. Two or more species can be co-dominants: for example, oak-ash woodland.
Dormant period*	A period of greatly reduced metabolism, in which a plant or part of a plant is alive but not actively growing.
Ecology	The study of the interrelationships between plants, animals and their environment – the human species included.
Ecosystem	A term used to describe a group of interdependent plants and animals and their environment.
Edaphic	Factors relating to the soil.
Evergreen	Tree or shrub which bears foliage throughout the year. Although it sheds leaves and produces new ones, the process is continuous, so that at no time is the plant devoid of foliage.

Feathered tree*	A tree generally 1.8–3.0m high with an upright, reasonably straight central leader and a stem furnished with evenly spread and balanced lateral shoots down to near ground level, according to its species. Feathered trees are designated according to their overall height, unless over 3m high, when the stem circumference at 1m above ground level is also specified. Feathered trees have been transplanted at least once in their life and their lateral growths may have been cut back to stimulate growth.
Feeding roots	Fine roots generally near to the surface of soil, which take up air, water and plant nutrients.
Forestry transplant*	A tree up to 1.2m high which has been undercut or transplanted at least once and is usually sold bare-rooted. Transplants are specified in terms of age, height and number of transplants or undercuts. The sizes most commonly used for amenity woodlands are 300–450mm and 450–600mm.
Form	The shape of a plant, including the arrangement of branches and leaves.
Frost pocket	An area where cold air collects, creating conditions where a frost is more likely to occur.
Frost-tender	Susceptible to damage by frost.
Genus*	A group of closely related species posessing certain characteristics in common, by which they are classified and distinguished from all others.
Germination*	The first stage in the development of a plant from a seed.
Ground cover*	A group of plants which, by their natural habit of low, close growth, are suitable for covering the ground surface and discouraging weeds.
Habitat	The environment in which a plant or animal lives.
Hardwood*	The timber derived from a broadleaved tree.
Herbaceous*	Non-woody plants. Herbaceous perennials die back to ground level each autumn, and grow again the following spring from an underground 'crown', whereas evergreen herbaceous plants retain their leaves throughout the year.
Herb layer	The layer of vegetation composed of annual, biennial and perennial herbaceous species, particularly in a woodland.
Hybrid*	A plant raised by the crossing of two genetically distinct plants. Hybrids may be between varieties (varietal), between species (specific) or, more rarely, between genera (generic). Such plants may either show a blending of characteristics from each parent of may favour one more than the other.
Hydraulic-seeding	Method of spreading a seed mixture by water pressure on to a steep slope or over a site which is inaccessible or unsuitable for normal cultivation.
Indigenous*	Plants originating in a particular locality, district, or country.

Inorganic fertilizer	Fertilizer manufactured from mineral-based chemicals.
Laying (of a hedge)	Traditional method of cutting, bending and interweaving hedge plants to produce a close, stockproof barrier.
Landscape management	Strategy and operations necessary for the long-term maintenance and development of a landscape scheme – for example, thinning of a forest plantation.
Leaching	The movement of soluble nutrients down through the soil in percolating rainwater.
Leaf litter	Layer of rotting leaves which eventually breaks down to form humus.
Macro-climate	The climate of a large geographical area – for example the south-west of England.
Maintenance	Routine operations necessary to keep a landscape scheme in good order – for example, pruning, mowing and weeding.
Mesoclimate	The climate of a local area which may differ from that of the region as a whole – for example, a river basin or coastal strip.
Micro-climate	Climate of a small area, such as an isolated hilltop, a walled garden or within a group of plants.
Monoculture	Cultivation of an extensive area of plants of a single species, either in agriculture or forestry.
Mowing margin	Hard strip laid between a built structure, such as a wall, and a grassed area, to simplify mowing.
Mowing regime	Number and frequency of grass cuts necessary each year to achieve the desired effect, usually defined by a minimum and maximum height.
Mulch	Leaf mould, forest bark, compost, well-rotted farmyard manure or similar organic material, spread over the soil surface around plants to conserve moisture and inhibit weed growth by restricting the light. Stones, gravel and synthetic sheet materials can also be used.
Native plant*	An indigenous plant.
Naturalized*	A plant which has been introduced to, and colonizes, places where it is not indigenous.
Natural regeneration	Regrowth of vegetation on an area of disturbed land. The variety of species that establish will depend on the adjacent seed source and the reservoir of seeds in the remaining soil on site.
Notch-planting	Method of planting a small tree in a notch cut by a spade. Used mainly for forestry plantings.
Nurse species	Quick-growing and expendable plants, grown to provide short-term protection for slower-growing species.
Organic fertilizer	Fertilizers derived from living matter – for example, fishmeal or bonemeal.
pH	Term used to express the measure of acidity or alkalinity of a solution.

Photosynthesis	Process by which plants use sunlight to convert carbon dioxide and water into carbohydrates. Oxygen is a by-product.
Pioneer species	The first plant species to colonize bare ground by self-seeding.
Plant nutrients	Mineral nutrients which are essential for plant growth.
'Pot-bound'	Plants whose roots have grown to fill the pot to the extent where further development is inhibited.
Pot-grown*	Plants which have been grown from seed or cuttings in a pot or similar container.
Pruning	Cutting back or thinning of a tree or shrub to produce the desired shape, or to encourage bushy growth or flowering.
Reduction of canopy	Cutting out carefully selected branches of a tree, to reduce the size or density of the canopy whilst retaining a balanced and characteristic shape.
Rhizome*	A prostrate thickened stem sending out roots and capable of producing leafy shoots and flowering stems from lateral and terminal buds. May also be a food storage organ, which can be used for plant propagation, as in the case of bearded irises.
Rootballed*	Plants grown in the open ground, and lifted with a well-defined ball of soil around the roots, usually wrapped in hessian or netting for protection.
Sapling*	A young tree. Usually used to describe young self-seeded trees.
'Sculptural' plant	Plant grown for its strong outline or the bold texture of its foliage.
Selective felling	Felling of individual trees within an area of forestry.
Selective weedkiller	Herbicide which kills only specific plants, rather than all plants.
Self-seeding	Plants which set seed and germinate freely.
Semi-mature*	A tree which is 6–15m high and 20–75cm girth and is normally transplanted with an intact, earth-bound rootball. The size and combined weight of tree (usually between 250kg and 10 tonne) plus earth necessitates the use of special equipment for lifting and replanting.
Shade-tolerant	Plants which will grow satisfactorily in the shade of buildings or other plants.
Shelter belt	A belt of trees and/or shrubs, planted where possible at right angles to the prevailing wind, to provide shelter by reducing windspeed.
Shrub*	A woody perennial with several stems from or near ground level.
Sightlines	Line of sight defining visibility splay to be kept clear at road junctions. Also line of sight defining parameters for forward visibility along a road.
Softwood*	Timber derived from conifers.
Soil erosion	Loss of soil, especially from a slope or unvegetated area by the action of water, gravity, ice and wind.

Species*	A subdivision of a genus consisting of plants which have the same constant and distinctive characters, and which have the capacity to interbreed amongst themselves.
Standard tree*	A tree 2.75–3.00m high, with a straight, clear stem of at least 1.8m below the lowest branch and a circumference of 8–10cm at 1.0m above ground level. A standard tree may be bare-root, root-balled or container-grown but it must have been transplanted at least once.
Subsoil	The soil below the topsoil layer, which is composed largely of mineral particles.
Subsoil drainage	Flow of water through the subsoil, either naturally, or through stone-filled or piped drains.
Succession	The sequence of plant communities that develop between the initial colonization of bare ground and the establishment of a stable climax vegetation. As this sequence unfolds, the plants themselves modify the physical environment, new species invade and the numbers of species and their proportions gradually change.
Sucker*	A shoot growing directly from an underground stem or root of a plant. Suckers are a normal growth characteristic of certain tree species, such as robinia and elm, but also arise from the parent rootstock of grafted or budded plants, especially roses.
Tap root	The first root produced by a seedling. Tap roots provide anchorage, growing straight down into the soil and bears lateral 'feeder' roots. Undercutting in the nursery severs the tap root and encourages the formation of a more fibrous root system.
Thinning	Removal of selected plants when they become overcrowded to encourage good form in remaining specimens by reducing competition for light, moisture and root space.
Tilth	Term used to describe soil which has been broken down into small particles by cultivation, to create suitable conditions for seed germination. Can only be achieved in suitable soil conditions.
Timber production	The planting and management of woodland to produce a tree crop which can be converted to marketable timber.
Top dressing	Addition of a fertilizer or soil improver to the soil surface or to grass.
Topiary	Cutting of hedges or shrubs into ornamental or unusual shapes.
Topsoil	Uppermost layers of soil, containing mineral nutrients and organic matter, organisms and plant roots. It is derived from weathering of subsoil and processes of decay and decomposition of plant and animal remains.
Trace elements	Mineral nutrients required in minute amounts for successful plant growth.

Tree*	Perennial woody plant which, in its natural state, has a distinct trunk or main stem and is usually taller than a shrub.
Tree canopy	An interwoven mass of branches and leaves above the clear stem of a tree.
Tree guard	Protection for individual newly planted trees from people, stock, rabbits and so on. Different types of guard are available for different functions.
Tree surgery	The cutting and treatment of limbs of a tree, to modify its shape or prolong its life span.
Tuber*	A short, thick, usually underground, modified stem, of one year's duration, in which food reserves are stored, and which usually has buds (eyes) from which new plants are produced.
Turfing	Establishment of grass area by laying turf onto a prepared bed.
Understorey	A layer of vegetation growing under groups of trees or shrubs.
Variegated	Leaf, stem or flower of more than one colour.
Variety*	A subdivision of species, consisting of plants which differ in some inherited characteristics, such as form, colour or season, from what is regarded as typical of the species. It is also applied to a member of a hybrid group.
Vegetation layers	Layers of herbs, shrubs and trees. These are well defined in the structure of a typical deciduous woodland.
Water table	A term used to describe the plane below which the soil or porous rock is completely saturated with water.
Weathering	The processes that disintegrate the surface of rocks, by physical, chemical or biological action.
Weed	Plant growing where it is not wanted.
Wind-chill factor	The cooling effect of the combination of wind and relatively low temperature on the body of an animal.

*Definitions based on:	BS 881 and 589 : 1974
	BS 3936 Part 1 : 1980
	BS 3936 Part 4 : 1984
	BS 3975 Part 4 : 1966
	BS 4043 : 1966
	BS 4428 : 1969
	BS 5236 : 1975

Bibliography

This bibliography has been prepared by Christine Smith of The Property Services Agency Library Services. As far as information was available, it was up to date as at February 1990. This bibliography does not claim to be a definitive list of all books available on Landscape Design, but gives a selection of those which might prove useful. Most of the publications cited are available in the United Kingdom.

Please note British Standards are listed at the end.

Allotments

Crouche, D. and Ward, C. (1988) *The Allotment: its landscape and culture.* London: Faber.

Bioengineering

Bache, D.H. and MacAskill, I.A. (eds) (1984) *Vegetation in civil and landscape engineering.* London: Granada. 317pp. (ISBN 0246115076).

Demonstrates the wide range of applications for vegetation as an engineering medium and evaluates its role in environmental control.

Stiles, R. (1988) 'Engineering with vegetation', *Landscape Design,* April, pp. 57–61.

Stresses the importance of the hitherto neglected science of bioengineering in the landscape.

Conservation

Conservation monitoring the management (1987) Cheltenham, Glos.: Countryside Commission.

Dodd, J. (1985) 'Landscape development for energy saving', *Construction,* vol. 52, Autumn, pp. 6–11.

Shows how the provision of well-designed external shelter can make the development site climate increase comfort, reduce wind damage and make worthwhile energy savings.

Poore, D. and J. (1987) *Protected Landscapes: the United Kingdom experience.* Cheltenham, Glos.: Countryside Commission.

Putwain, P.D. and Gillham, D.A. (1988) 'Restoration of heather moorland', *Landscape Design,* April, pp. 51–6.

Explains a seven-year experiment to restore heather moorland destroyed by china-clay waste heaps.

Disabled

Goldsmith, S. (1984, updated edn) *Designing for the disabled.* RIBA Publications. 525pp. (ISBN 0900630507).

Gives anthropometric and measurement information, building elements and finishes, services, installations, general spaces, public buildings and housing.

Thorpe, Stephen (1986) *Designing for people with sensory impairments.* Centre on Environment for the Handicapped. 21pp. (ISBN 090397617).

Aims to provide guidance for designers of public buildings and spaces for people with sensory impairments. Also for planning outdoor spaces, new building design, and adaptation of existing buildings, and to assist all those whose work affects the quality of the built environment to go beyond meeting statutory obligations and respond to the needs of people with sensory impairments.

Ecology

Johnston, M. (1983) 'Urban trees and an ecological approach to urban landscape design', *Arboricultural Journal,* November, pp. 275–82.

Madders, M. and Laurence, M. (1981) 'Air pollution control by vegetation buffer zones', *Landscape Design,* August, pp. 29–31.

McHarg, I.L. (1969) *Design with nature.* New York: Natural History Press.

Provides an ecological viewpoint to the design of landscape in urban and rural areas.

Fences

see also Hedges, Shelterbelts, Walls and BS 1722

British Trust for Conservation Volunteers (1986) *Fencing: a practical conservation handbook.* Wallingford 141 pp. (ISBN 0946752044).

Practical, comprehensive information is provided for design and siting, safety, strained fencing (materials and construction), wooden and electric fencing and gates and stiles.

Central Electricity Generating Board (1965) *Design memorandum on the use of fences.* 36pp.

Diagrams illustrate the use of fences, barriers, walls and hedges which form important visual effects in a landscape.

Jaffa, G. (1985) 'Fencing requirements in the eyes of the law', *Parks and Sports Grounds,* January, pp. 10–11.

Historic boundaries, maintenance rights.

Pepper, H.Q. and Tee, L.A. (1986) *Forest fencing.* 2nd edn. London: HMSO, Forestry Commission Leaflet no. 87. 42pp.

Discusses fence components and associated tools, fence construction and maintenance, and the principles and specification for fencing.

Follies and Pavilions

Headley, B. and Meulenkamp, W. (1986) *Follies: A National Trust Guide.* London: Jonathan Cape. xxviii. 564pp (ISBN 0224021052).

Describes structures erected in complete disregard for building practices, or tastes, on impossible sites with no easy access, with costs out of proportion to their use. These structures may well add interest to the landscape.

Jones, B. (1974) *Follies and grottoes.* London: Constable. 459pp. (ISBN 0094593507).

Describes follies and grottoes and shows how they may enhance a landscape.

Smith, J. Abel (1978) *Pavilions in peril.* Ed. by Sophie Andreae. SAVE Britain's Heritage. 40pp. (ISBN 0905978234).

Considers various garden accessories in danger – pavilions, gazebos, grottoes, garden buildings of various types. Also describes the gardens and historic houses and grounds where these items may be located.

Footbridges

Footbridges in the Countryside: design and construction (1981) Perth: Countryside Commission for Scotland. 101pp. (ISBN 0902226525).

Illustrates in detail aspects of footbridge selection, design, construction and maintenance.

Forestry

see also Trees and Woodland

Campbell, D. (1987) 'Landscape design in forestry', *Landscape Design,* April, pp. 31–3, 35–6.

The Forestry Commission's landscape architects reflect on the development of their landscape policy over the past twenty-five years.

Forestry in the Countryside (1987) Cheltenham, Glos.: Countryside Commission. CCP 245. (ISBN 0861701976).

Describes the role the Commission thinks forestry should play in the countryside. It makes a number of recommendations for action by government and other agencies and outlines a number of initiatives which the Commission proposes to take.

Garden Design

Brookes, J. (1979) *Room outside: a new approach to garden design.* London: Thames and Hudson. 256pp. (ISBN 0500271372).

Covers design, ground shaping and drainage, enclosure, hard surfacing, soft ground surfacing, skeleton planting, planting design, garden furnishings, special features such as water, rockeries.

Brookes, J. (1989) *The new small garden book*. London: Dorling Kindersley Limited. 224pp. (ISBN 0863183484).

A comprehensive look at the variety of designs possible for small areas and the use of plants.

Brown, J. (1986) *The English garden in our time from Gertrude Jekyll to Geoffrey Jellicoe*. Woodbridge, Suffolk: Antique Collectors Club. 272pp. (ISBN 1851490124).

Looks at twentieth-century garden design. Includes sections on the Arts and Crafts Movement, the Italian influence, the Modern Movement, 'New Georgian' gardens and the work of Sir Geoffrey Jellicoe.

Crowe, S. (1981) *Garden design*. Packard Publishing. 224pp. (ISBN 0906527058).

Presents a history of design in gardens and examines the need for these principles to be applied to the contemporary landscape.

Elliott, B. (1986) *Victorian gardens*. London: B.T. Batsford. 285pp. (ISBN 071344763X).

Victorian gardens resulted from rebellion against eighteenth century landscape parks. Gives the history of the Victorian gardening movement, creation of jobs, design, art and nature, conservatories, carpet bedding, the use of colour. Also remarks on Dutch, Italian and Old English gardens. Includes Edwardian gardens.

Jellicoe, G. and S. (eds) (1986) *The Oxford companion to gardens*. OUP. 651pp. (ISBN 0198661231).

Over 1500 entries embracing articles from history of garden design to short definitions of terms. Individual entries for 700 gardens – layout, special characteristics and significance. Biographical entries for designers, gardeners, plant collectors and garden enthusiasts.

Paul, A. and Rees, Y. (1988) *The garden design book*. London: Collins.

Selected garden designers consider their philosophy and reviews certain of their designs.

The Sunday Times (1983) *The making of the English garden*. London: Macmillan.

Titchmarsh, A. (1988) *The concise encyclopaedia of gardening techniques*. London: Mitchell Beazley.

Triggs, H.I. (1988) *Formal gardens in England and Scotland*. Woodbridge, Suffolk: Antique Collectors Club.

Turner, T. (1986) *English garden design: history and styles since 1650*. Woodbridge, Suffolk: Antique Collectors Club. 238pp. (ISBN 0907462251).

Covers the background ideas: the period 1650–1740 which discusses the enclosed French and Dutch styles; 1714–1810 includes the Forest, Serpentine and irregular styles; 1794–1870 covers the Transition, Italian and Mixed styles; 1870–1985 embraces the Arts and Crafts and Abstract styles and includes recent trends.

Greenbelts

Elson, M. (1986) *Green belts: conflict mediation in the urban fringe*. London: Heinemann. (ISBN 0434905321).

Planning for countryside in Metropolitan areas (1987) Cheltenham, Glos.: Countryside Commission.

Hedges

see also Fences, Shelterbelts and Walls

British Trust for Conservation Volunteers (1988) *Hedging: a practical conservation handbook*. Comp. by A. Brooks; 3rd rev. edn. by E. Agate. Wallingford, Oxford. 120pp. (ISBN 0946752628).

Deals with farm hedges, hedges with a practical purpose, and hedges which are stock fences or shelter plantings. Explains different methods of regional styles of hedge laying and discusses choice of plant species, planting and various methods of management.

Hedge management (1980) Cheltenham, Glos.: Countryside Commission. Leaflet no. 7. (ISBN 0902590977).

History of Landscape

Hoskins, W.G. (1988) *The making of the English landscape*. Sevenoaks, Kent: Hodder. (ISBN 0340399716).

Describes the English landscape through the ages.

Jellicoe, G. and S. (1987) *The landscape of man: Shaping the environment from prehistory to the present day*. London: Thames and Hudson. 400pp. (ISBN 0500274312).

A concise globai view of the designed landscape past and present, with 734 illustrations.

Industrial Landscape

Crowe, S. (1958) *The landscape of power*. Architectural Press. 115pp.

Power stations, hydroelectric power, oil, airfields, power and national parks.

Tandy, C. (1975) *Landscape of industry*. New York/London: John Wiley. 314pp. (ISBN 047084440X).

Concerned with the impact of industry on the landscape in the past, the present and the future. Looks at the damage which has been done to the environment by industry and studies methods by which this damage can be rectified.

Land Classification

Landscape assessment of farmland (1988) Cheltenham, Glos.: Countryside Commission.

Tansley, Sir A.G. (1965) *The British Islands and their vegetation.* Cambridge: University Press. 2 vols. (ISBN 052106600X).

Chapters on the nature and classification of vegetation including woodland, grassland, fen, marsh and bog vegetation, heath and moor, and marine vegetation.

Land Reclamation

Bradshaw, A.D. and Chadwick, M.J. (1980) *The restoration of land.* Oxford: Blackwell. (ISBN 0632091800).

Deals with the problems of derelict land on a global scale and shows how the problems can be solved most effectively through a scientific understanding of the ecological factors which affect plant growth.

Cairney, T. (ed.) 1987) *Reclaiming contaminated land.* Glasgow: Blackie & Son Ltd. 272pp. (ISBN 021691874X).

Chapters cover: recognition of the problem; types of contaminated land; main types of contaminants; appropriate site investigations; available reclamation methods; soil cover reclamations; long-term monitoring of reclaimed sites; safety in site reclamation; policy planning and financial issues; landscaping and vegetating reclaimed sites; hazards from methane and carbon monoxide.

Land Use

The changing landscape (1988) Cheltenham, Glos.: Countryside Commission.

Landscape Institute (1985) *Farmed landscapes: A balanced future.* Landscape Institute. 32pp.

Advocates the creation by the government of a countryside register and management scheme in order to preserve a balance between conservation and the agricultural use of land.

New opportunities for the countryside (1987) Cheltenham, Glos.: Countryside Commission.

Stamp, L.D. (1962) *The land of Britain: its use and misuse.* 3rd edn. London: Longmans. 545pp.

Land use, soils, farming.

Landscape Architects

Harvey, S. (ed.) (1987) *Reflections on landscape: The lives and work of six British landscape architects.* Aldershot: Gower. 155pp. (ISBN 0291397085).

Based on interviews, this book includes chapters on: Sir Geoffrey Jellicoe, Dame Sylvia Crowe, Sir Peter Shepheard, Brian Hackett, Peter Youngman and Brenda Colvin.

Landscape Design

see also BS 1192 : Part 4, BS 4428

Aldous, T. and Clouston, B. (1979) *Landscape by design.* London: Heinemann. 173pp. O/P (ISBN 0434018058).

Outlines the development of the landscape profession in Great Britain since the foundation of the Landscape Institute in 1929. The background, aims and results of main landscape schemes for new towns, industry and local authorities are discussed.

Alpern, A. (1982) *Handbook of speciality elements in architecture.* Maidenhead, Berks: McGraw-Hill. 484pp. (ISBN 0070013608).

Deals with the special features that make buildings both functionally and aesthetically distinctive: exterior lighting; interior and exterior trees and plants; works of art; pools and fountains; signage; audiovisual communications; and accommodation for the disabled.

Austin, R.L. (1984) *Designing the natural landscape.* London: Van Nostrand Reinhold. 117pp. (ISBN 0442209789).

A practical sourcebook providing specifications for planting trees, shrubs and vines, design criteria for water features, standards and specifications for the development of wildlife habitats and case studies of individual landscape projects.

Booth, N.K. (1983) *Basic elements of landscape architectural design.* Barking, Essex: Elsevier. 315pp. (ISBN 0444007660).

Considers the significance and potential uses of landform, plant materials, buildings, pavement, site structures and water in landscape architecture.

Colvin, B. (1970) *Land and landscape: evolution design and control.* 2nd edn. London: John Murray. 414pp. O/P (ISBN 0719518008).

Covers landscape development, principles and practice of design.

Evans, B.M. (ed.) 1984) *Proceedings of the 'Greenchips' symposium on computer-aided landscape design: Principles and practice,* University of Strathclyde, 1983. Scotland: Landscape Institute. 165pp. (ISBN 0950961302).

Fairbrother, N. (1974) *The nature of landscape design.* New York: Alfred A. Knopf. 252pp. (ISBN 039447046X).

Hannebaum, L. (1981) *Landscape design: A practical approach.* Reston Publishing Company. 392pp. (ISBN 0835939340).

Provides information on landscape design, the study of land forms, environmental design, drainage of surface and subsurface water and retaining wall design.

Ingels, J.E. (1983) *The landscape book.* 2nd edn. London: Van Nostrand Reinhold. 273pp. (ISBN 0442242174).

Practical information on the basic principles of landscape design, construction, materials and maintenance.

Landphair, H.C. and Klatt, F. (1988) *Landscape architecture construction.* Barking, Essex: Elsevier. 433pp. (ISBN 0444012869).

Emphasizes the creative use of technology through an awareness of the alternatives among available tools and construction processes.

Laurie, M. (1986) *An introduction to landscape architecture.* 2nd edn. Barking, Essex: Elsevier. 248pp. (ISBN 044409701)

Deals with various aspects of landscape architecture and how it has developed over recent years. Covers ecological analysis, conservation and landscape planning.

Simonds, J.O. (1983) *Landscape architecture: A manual of site planning and design.* New York: McGraw-Hill. 331pp. (ISBN 0070574480).

Information on site, visual aspects of plan arrangement and structures in the landscape.

Tregay, R. and Gustavsson, R. (1983) *Oakwood's new landscape: Designing for nature in the residential environment.* Warrington and Runcorn Development Corporation. (ISBN 9157614504).

Oakwood's new landscape is seen as one of the most thorough examples of an ecological approach to landscape development in England. Describes the main principles and ideas during the construction period.

Weddle, A.E. (1979) *Landscape techniques.* London: Heinemann. 265pp. (ISBN 0434922277).

Describes the range of techniques that can be used by the landscape architect. Covers conservation and management of the coastline, ground modelling, trees and planting, turf, maintenance practices.

Landscape Planning

see also Conservation

Dodd. J. (1989) 'Greenscape', *Architects Journal*, April–May.

Hackett, B. (1971) *Landscape planning: an introduction to theory and practice.* Oriel Press. 124pp. (ISBN 0853621209).

Landscape planning techniques, ecology, aesthetics, conservation and recreation.

Jacobs, J. (1977) *Death and life of great American cities.* Harmondsworth: Penguin Books. 474pp. (ISBN 0140206817).

Deals with failures in town planning – good ideas that went wrong.

Lynch, K. and Hack, G. (1984) *Site planning.* 3rd edn. Cambridge, Mass./London: MIT Press. 499pp. (ISBN 0262121069).

The introductory chapter summarizes the site planning process and subsequent chapters provide a case study of a typical project covering such topics as user analysis, programming, design strategies, mapping and environmental impact analysis.

Turner, T. (1987) *Landscape planning*. London: Hutchinson. 213pp. (ISBN 009164710X).

> Covers landscape theory and landscape of industry, reservoirs, mines, quarries, parks, forestry, flood control, housing, new towns, and the renewal of the urban landscape.

Landscape Practice

Clamp, H. (1988) *The shorter forms of building contract*. 2nd edn. Oxford: BSP Professional Books. 170pp. (ISBN 0632018437).

> Concentrates on the 1980 JCT Form of Building Agreement for Minor Works but also surveys a range of other shorter forms.

Clamp, H. (ed.) (1986) *Spon's landscape contract manual: A guide to good practice and procedures in the management of landscape contracts*. London: Spon. 195pp. (ISBN 0419134808).

Lovejoy, D. & Partners (eds.) (1986) *SPON's Landscape handbook*. 3rd edn. London: Spon. 470pp. (ISBN 0419133801).

> Covers fees; town planning; site investigations; use of trees; data collection and landscape drawings; computer-aided design and information technology; specifications for siteworks; soft landscape works; hard landscape works; sports and recreation; water features; street and garden furniture; mechanical plant. Includes bibliography, list of manufacturers and suppliers.

Lovejoy, D. & Partners (eds.) (annual) *SPON's Landscape and external works price book*. London: Spon.

> Covers all items needed for a medium-sized hard and soft landscape contract; recent legislation, fees and preliminaries, prices for measured work, approximate estimates.

Legislation

Harte, J.D.C. (1985) *Landscape, land use and the law*. London: Spon. 450pp. (ISBN 0419125108).

> Provides comprehensive treatment of land boundaries, legal arrangements for controlling the use of land and legal responsibilities.

Heap, D. (1987) *Outline of planning law*. 9th edn. London: Sweet & Maxwell. (ISBN 0421354402).

> Focuses on plans and control of development, public enquiries.

Lighting

see also BS 873

Bell, J. (1987) 'Lighting the landscape', *Landscape Design*, December, pp.58–60.

> Describes what to look for in lighting projects.

Caminada, J.F. (1987) 'Lighting in residential areas', *Landscape Design*, December, pp.61–5.

Places emphasis on the safety and social aspects of residential lighting.

Cassidy, D. (1988) 'Shedding some light ...', *Landscape Design*, April, pp. 40–4.

Use of lighting in landscape design.

Dodds, B. 'Lighting design – and art form', *Landscape Design*, February, pp. 50–2.

Describes the importance of site-specific lighting, quoting the unusual example of the Queen Elizabeth Hospital, Alberta, Canada.

Electricity Council (1983) *Outdoor lighting.* Electricity Council. 36pp.

Sets out to encourage the effective and imaginative use of exterior lighting, with due regard to the wise use of energy. It considers building floodlighting, sports lighting, security lighting, and advertising.

Harvey, S. (comp.) (1988) 'Lighting bibliography', *Landscape Design*, April, p.45.

Lighting Industry Federation (1980) *Lamp guide.* London: Lighting Industry Federation. 11pp.

Reviews the basic types of lamp and explains their different characteristics.

Lovejoy, D. (1988) 'Light on the roads', *Landscape Design*, February, pp.53–6.

Considers the special problems associated with lighting motorways and major roads.

Open Spaces

Lambert, C.M. (comp.) (1981) *Urban open spaces: A select list of material based on the DOE/DTp library.* Department of the Environment. Library Bibliography no. 956. 52pp. (ISBN 0718401824).

Parks

Design Council (1979) *Equipment for parks and amenity areas.* Design Council. 114pp. (ISBN 0850720834).

A catalogue of equipment for parks and amenity areas that have been chosen by the Council's Street Furniture Advisory Committee for their high standard of design.

Wright, T. (1982) *Large gardens and parks, maintenance, management and design.* London: Granada. 194pp. (ISBN 0246114029).

Covers contemporary garden management, design, restoration of neglected or abandoned gardens and maintenance of historic gardens.

Paving – General

see also Pedestrian Areas and BS 340, BS 6677

Beazley, E. (1960) *Design and detail of the space between buildings.* Architectural Press. 230pp.

Includes paved spaces, trim of paved spaces, walls and fences and planning.

Bolton, H. (1988) 'Setting the street in Norwich', *Landscape Design,* October, pp.27–31.

Describes the details of paving and design in the revitalized pedestrian scheme in Norwich city centre.

Department of the Environment (1970) *A guide to the structural design of pavements for new roads.* Third edn. London: HMSO. 36pp. Road Research Laboratory: Road Note 29. O/P. (ISBN 0115501584).

Guide to hard landscape. (1986) Architects Journal Supplement 26 November.

Sponsored by the Brick Development Association (BDA), the supplement deals with reworking existing town centre developments; promoting new schemes such as science parks where landscape is an important factor. Includes lighting landscape; use of blocks and pavers; freestanding and retaining walls.

Howcroft, H. (1988) 'The techniques of sett laying', *Landscape Design,* October, pp.46–9.

Provides basic guidelines.

National Paving and Kerb Association (1984) *Paving flags: The product selector: to BS 368.* Folder.

Leaflets entitled: Techniques for laying; Small element paving flags, paving for the blind.

Scottish Local Authorities Special Housing Group (1975) *External environment. Hard surfaces: edging.* Edinburgh: SLASH Research Unit. pag. var.

Covers design, materials and their properties, bonding patterns, component drawings and standard details and preambles.

Tandy, C. (ed.) (1978) *Handbook of urban landscape.* Architectural Press. Paperback edn. First published 1972. 275pp. (ISBN 0851396917).

Section 10 'Elements of landscape construction' includes information sheets on surface treatments and pavings.

Paving – Brick

see also BS 187, BS 3921

Brick Development Association (1984) *Brick pavements.* 11pp.

Illustrated guide to the design and construction of flexible brick pavements.

Hammett, M. (1988) 'A new look at an old material', *Landscape Design,* October, pp. 39–43.

Reviews present practice and use of brick in the design of paving and walls.

Handisyde, C. (1976) *Hard landscape in brick.* Architectural Press. 72pp. (ISBN 0851392830).

Detailed, illustrated guidance on the use of brick for paving and as a landscape material.

Paving – Clay and Calcium Silicate

see also BS 6677

Brick Development Association (1988) *Specification for clay pavers for flexible pavements.* Brick Development Association with the co-operation of the County Surveyors' Society. 8pp.

Cook, I.D. (1981) *Flexible clay and calcium silicate paving for lightly trafficked roads and paved areas.* Brick Development Association. Design Note: no. 5. 8pp.

Contains design guidance and practical laying recommendations for flexible pavements of clay and calcium silicate. Applies to the design of lightly trafficked pavements intended to carry no more than 1.5 million standard (8200 kg) axles during their design lives.

Hammett, M. and Smith, R.A. (1984) *Rigid paving with clay and calcium silicate.* Brick Development Association. 15pp.

Deals mainly with paving out-of-doors and covers the laying of pavers on a mortar bed and with a mortar joint between each joint.

Smith, R. (1988) *Code of practice for flexible pavements constructed in clay pavers.* Brick Development Association. 8pp.

Smith, R.A. (1985) *Flexible paving with clay and calcium silicate pavers.* Brick Development Association. 32pp.

Paving – Cobble

Downing, M.F. (1977) *Landscape construction.* London: Spon. 247pp. (ISBN 0419108904).

Use of cobbles as a paving material given in pages 152–3.

Howarth, M. (1988) 'The art of cobblestones', *Landscape Design,* October, pp. 34–7.

Calls for a new look at an old tradition and shows some of the exciting modern cobblestone designs.

Paving – Concrete

see also BS 6717

Cement and Concrete Association (1983) *Code of practice for laying precast concrete paving blocks.* Cement and Concrete Association: County Surveyors Society and Interlocking Paving Association (Interpave). 7pp. (ISBN 072101285X).

Duell, J. (1981) 'Products in practice: External paving – product selection and specification', *Architects Journal,* vol. 173, no. 18, 6 May, pp.861–9.

Compares different types of concrete and clay units for jointed external paving. Provides information on sizes, patterns and gives notes on the detailing and installation.

Lilley, A.A. and Collins, J.R. (1984) *Laying concrete block paving.* Cement and Concrete Association. 15pp.

Maynard, D.M. (1983) *In situ concrete for industrial paving.* Cement and Concrete Association. Design Guide. 7pp. (ISBN 0721013007).

The design guide is for engineers, architects and contractors concerned with the design, supervision and construction of concrete paving for external industrial uses.

Pritchard, C. (1988) 'Concrete block paving', *Landscape Design,* October, pp. 50–3.

Describes quality, uses, design and layout.

Paving – Mastic Asphalt

Mastic Asphalt Council and Employers Federation (1980) *Paving handbook.* 20pp.

Provides guidance on the use of mastic asphalt in a variety of paving applications.

Paving – Stone

Booth, N.K. (1983) *Basic elements of landscape architectural design.* Barking, Essex: Elsevier. 315pp. (ISBN 0444007660).

Considers the significance and potential uses of landform, plant materials, buildings, pavements, site structures and water in landscape architecture. Pages 190–4 deal with stone setts.

Natural Stone Directory 1985: Dimension stone sources for Britain and Ireland/ Stone Industries. (1985) Ealing Publications. 124pp.

Includes sections on durability assessment, the stone of Britain, index to UK and Irish active quarries, stones grouped by colour, stone tracer (materials now unavailable), materials source guide, masonry training facilities.

Pedestrian Areas

see also Paving, Urban Landscape

Morgan, N. (1988) 'Pedestrianised zones in urban areas', *Landscape Design*, October, pp.24–6.

A case study reveals the influence of landscape architects and calls for greater imagination and creativity.

Plant Selection

see also BS 3975

Brickell, C.B. (ed.) (1980) *International code of nomenclature for cultivated plants.* Bohn, Scheltema, Holkema, Utrecht, The Netherlands. Regnum Vegetabilae, vol. 104. 32pp. (ISBN 9031304468).

Ferguson, N. (1984) *Garden plant directory: the essential guide to planning your garden.* London: Pan Books. 292pp. (ISBN 0330265946).

Illustrates more than 1400 plants and for each plant gives botanical and common name, height, flowering season, flower colour, important and individual characteristics.

Grouter, W. (ed.) (1988) *International code of botanical nomenclature.* Federal Republic of Germany: Koelz Scientific Books. i-xiv. Regnum Vegetabilae Series. 328pp. (ISBN 3874292789).

Joint Liaison Committee on Plant Supplies (1981) *Herbaceous plants: exotic and British native.* Horticultural Trades Association. 28pp.

Gives the best growth conditions for each type of plant.

Joint Liaison Committee on Plant Supplies (no date) *Plant list: trees, shrubs, conifers.* Reading: Horticultural Trades Association.

Keble Martin, W. (1986) *The concise British flora in colour.* 4th edn. by J. Taylor. London: Michael Joseph. 254pp. (ISBN 0718127005).

Glossary, detailed botanical descriptions and illustrations.

Maddison, Alan (1985) 'A modern approach to computerised plant selection (Computers in landscape practice)', *Landscape Design*, June, pp.37–8.

Program facilities, hardware and software for a landscape practice.

Philip, C. and Lord, T. (comps) (1987) *The plant finder.* Headmain for the Hardy Plant Society. 450pp. (ISBN 0951216104).

Lists over 22,000 plants available from some 300 nurseries.

Rice, G. (1988) *Plants for problem places.* Bromley, Kent: Christopher Helm.

Spencer-Jones, D. and Wade, M. (1986) *Aquatic plants: a guide to recognition.* ICI Professional products. 169pp. (ISBN 0901747033).

Sturgess, P. (1985) 'Plant health and maintenance' *Landscape Design*, October, p.41.

Reports on the important growth in the understanding of plant health and maintenance.

Thomas, G.S. (1977) *Plants for ground cover.* Dent and Royal Horticultural Society. 282pp. (ISBN 0460039946).

Covers shrubs, climbing plants, conifers, herbaceous plants, grasses, rushes, ferns, annuals and biennials.

Planting

see also BS 3882, BS 5236

Austin, R.L. (1982) *Designing with plants.* London: Van Nostrand Reinhold. 190pp. (ISBN 0442246587).

Illustrations and diagrams accompany text on the ecology of planting design, analysis and implementation.

Beckett, K. and G. (1979) *Planting native trees and shrubs.* Jarrold. 64p.

Gives advice on what to plant and where to plant it, and how to raise trees and shrubs from seeds or cuttings.

Carpenter, P.L. and others (1975) *Plants in the landscape.* Oxford: W.H. Freeman. 481pp. (ISBN 0716707780).

An introduction to the principles and practices of ornamental horticulture in landscape architecture. Covers the history and development of landscape design and details of landscape contracting.

Clouston, B. (ed.) (1977) *Landscape design with plants.* London: Heinemann. 456pp. (ISBN 0434366501).

Includes designing with trees, forest planting, herbaceous plants and bulbs and also covers the technical aspects of planting in special conditions such as on spoiled land or in conditions of air pollution.

Cotton, S. (1988) *Guide to the specialist nurseries and garden suppliers in Britain and Ireland.* Woodbridge, Suffolk: Antique Collectors Club.

Hackett, B. (1979) *Planting design.* London: Spon. 174pp. (ISBN 0419127305).

Sets out the visual, ecological and economic principles of planting and provides a logical basis for the planting of particular trees, shrubs and other plants in different environments.

The planting and aftercare of trees and shrubs. (1979) Cheltenham, Glos.: Countryside Commission. Leaflet no. 3 (ISBN 0902590766).

Plants and Planting Methods for the Countryside. Perth: Countryside Commission for Scotland. Information Sheets.

A series of information sheets containing comprehensive advice on tree and shrub planting, on choice of species, and on the management of vegetation in some particular recreation areas such as beaches, and loch shores.

Pryce, S. (1988) 'Colourful and cheerful bedding displays', *Landscape Design*, February, pp.39–42.

Describes the variety of bedding plants now available and suggests ways in which landscape designers can use them to create colourful and interesting displays.

Roberts, D. and Bradshaw, A. (1986) 'Hydraulic seeding', *Landscape Design*, August, pp.42–7.

Hydroseeding can be a very economic and successful method of seeding steep slopes or inaccessible areas of topsoil, raw subsoil and derelict land material.

Thomas, G.S. (1984) *The art of planting.* Dent with National Trust. 323pp. (ISBN 0460046403).

Covers garden schemes (colour, styles of planting), plants, garden features and a list of plants for special purposes.

Play/Playgrounds

see also BS 5696

Baker, B. (1987) *Sports and play surfaces and associated equipment dictionary-directory.* Barry Baker Publications. 180pp.

An alphabetical list of terminology, products and firms relating to the construction of sports surfaces.

Heseltine, P. and Holborn, J. (1987) *Playgrounds: the planning, design and construction of play environments.* London: Mitchell Beazley. 204pp. (ISBN 0713452226).

Covers importance and development of playspace, playgrounds, installation, site design, planting and management.

Moore, R.C. (1986) *Childhood's domain, play and place in child development.* London: Croom Helm. 311pp. (ISBN 0856649368).

Explores children's habitats and looks at ways of conserving and creating childhood domains.

National Playing Fields Association (1987) *Impact absorbing surfaces.* London. 34pp. (ISBN 094608517X).

Describes the surfaces available and discusses their advantages and disadvantages, their ability to absorb the impact of a falling child and guidance on their installation.

National Playing Fields Association (1987) *Insurance for children's play.* London. 12pp. (ISBN 0946085145).

National Playing Fields Association (1988) *Playground equipment manufacturers list.* London. 7pp.

National Playing Fields Association (1987) *Playground management for local councils.* 2nd edn. London. 68pp. (ISBN 0946085161).

Looks at legal and insurance responsibilities and design considerations; inspection and maintenance procedures for playgrounds. Also includes an illustrated inspection guide to help identify common equipment faults.

National Playing Fields Association (1987) *Suppliers of impact absorbing surfaces for children's play areas.* London. 13pp.

Recreation

Equipment and Materials for Countryside Recreation Sites. Perth: Countryside Commission for Scotland. Information Sheets.

A series of information sheets available singly or in two ring binders, giving details on the construction, design and manufacturers of materials and products such as litter bins, gates, stiles, picnic furniture, etc., associated with recreation sites in the countryside.

Roads

see also BS 594, BS 1447, BS 4987, BS 5273

Crowe, S. (1960) *The landscape of roads.* Architectural Press. 136pp.

Emphasizes that road design and construction need qualified planners, architects and landscape architects and highway engineers in order to be absorbed naturally into the existing landscape pattern.

Department of the Environment (1977) *Parking in new housing schemes.* DOE Housing Development Notes VII (Parts 1 and 2). 24pp.

Covers levels of provision, planning and car space density and general requirements.

Department of the Environment (1977) *Residential roads and footpaths: Layout considerations.* London: HMSO. Design Bulletin no.32. 78pp. (ISBN 011750243X).

Considers effective provision for offstreet parking and pedestrian movement.

Department of Transport (1976) *Specification for road and bridge works.* 5th edn. London: HMSO. 194pp. O/P. (ISBN 0115503749). Supplement no. 1, 1978. 66pp. O/P. (ISBN 0115504753).

Design Council (1979) *Streets ahead.* 111pp. (ISBN 0850720818).

Stresses the mutual responsibility of planners, architects, businessmen, and shopkeepers in creating the street scene. Includes notes on the selection and siting of street furniture. Vandalism, signing systems, problems of cars in residential areas, advertising and shop front design come within the parameter of the book.

McCluskey, J. (1979) *Road form and townscape.* London: Architectural Press. 310pp. (ISBN 0851395481).

Covers the essentials of road engineering whilst bringing attention to the environmental context within which roads must be planned and built if they are to succeed with the people who have to use and live among them.

Shelterbelts

see also Fences and Walls

Ministry of Agriculture, Fisheries and Food (1977) *Shelterbelts for farmland.* London: HMSO. 27pp. (ISBN 0112406114).

Practical advice is given on the design, siting, establishment and maintenance of windbreaks with notes on the most suitable tree and shrub species for different conditions.

Ministry of Agriculture, Fisheries and Food (1979) *Windbreaks.* London. 39pp.

Provides practical details on windbreaks for a variety of purposes, eg for nursery stock, glasshouses. Advantages and disadvantages are discussed.

Patch, D. and Lines, R. (1981) *Winter shelter for agricultural stock.* Farnham, Surrey: Forestry Commission. 3pp. (Arboriculture Research Note 35/81/ SILN)

Signs

see also BS 873

Brown, A.C.H. (1974) *The construction and design of signs in the countryside.* Perth: Countryside Commission for Scotland. 41pp. (ISBN 0902226193).

The results of a study concerned with collecting, rationalizing and presenting information on the design of signs.

Street Furniture

Design Council (1979) *Street furniture.* Design Council. 192pp. (ISBN 0850720826).

A catalogue of products chosen by the Street Furniture Advisory Council for their high standard of design. Particular subjects covered are: street lighting; seating; planting; shelters and kiosks; and poster display units.

Gay, J. (1985) *Cast-iron: architecture and ornament, function and fantasy.* London: J. Murray. 112pp. (ISBN 0719542308).

A look at cast-iron as an element in architecture, verandahs, balconies, railings, gates, conservatories, decoration.

Littlewood, M. (1986) *Landscape detailing.* Architectural Press. 214pp. (ISBN 085139860X).

Comprises thirteen sections, ranging from free-standing walls to fences and gates, steps and ramps, drainage channels and tree surrounds. Each section begins with the technical guidance notes on design and specification followed by a set of drawn-to-scale sheets plus specification notes.

Thwaites, K. (1988) 'A reassessment of standards', *Landscape Design,* December, pp.15–17.

Calls for a revolution in the design and marketing of artefacts available for landscape work.

Warren, G. (1978) *Vanishing street furniture.* Newton Abbot: David & Charles. 159pp. (ISBN 0715374826).

Covers the development of such public utilities as street lighting, drinking fountains, water closets, milestones, etc., from earliest times to the Edwardian period, concentrating on the nineteenth century.

Timber

see also BS 881 and BS 589

Timber Research and Development Association (1985) *Preservative treatment for timber – a guide to specification.* High Wycombe: TRADA. 2pp.

Timber Research and Development Association (1987) *Timbers – their properties and uses.* High Wycombe: TRADA. 8pp.

The treatment of exterior timber against decay (1987) 2nd edn. Perth: Countryside Commission for Scotland. 24pp. (ISBN 0902226681).

Describes the causes and control of timber decay. It covers the role of preservatives, paints, varnishes, oils and exterior stain finishes.

Trees

see also BS 3936, BS 3998, BS 4043, BS 5236, BS 5837

Arboricultural Association (1983) *Trees in the 21st century.* Based on the First International Arboricultural Conference sponsored by the Arboricultural Association in conjunction with the International Association of Arboriculture. Berkhampsted, Herts: AB Academic Publishers. 133pp.

Papers on conservation policies to combat the destruction of large forests, the effect on landscapes of changing agricultural policies, urban development, disease and drought.

Arnold, H.F. (1980) *Trees in urban design.* New York/London: Van Nostrand Reinhold. 168pp. (ISBN 0442203365).

Advocates a fresh approach to the use of trees in urban environments. Design based on classical principles of grouping trees rather than scattering and is illustrated with regard to American cities. Individual species are assessed as to their suitability in landscape design.

Bean, W.J. (1970–1980) *Trees and shrubs hardy in the British Isles.* London: John Murray. vol. 1 A–C 8th edn. by G. Taylor, 1970 (ISBN 0719517907); vol. 2 D–M 8th edn. by G. Taylor, 1973 (ISBN 0719522560); vol. 3 N–Rh 8th edn. by D.L. Clarke and G. Taylor, 1976 (ISBN 071952427X); vol. 4 Ri–Z 8th edn. by D.L. Clarke and G. Taylor, 1980 (ISBN 0719524288).

Provides detailed descriptions.

Bean, W.J. (1988) *Trees and shrubs hardy in the British Isles.* Ed. D.L. Clarke. 8th rev. edn. Supplement to vols I–IV. London: John Murray. 616pp. (ISBN 0719544432).

Biddle, P.G. (1985) 'Arboricultural implications of revision of National House-Building Council: Practice Note 3 – Building near trees', *Arboricultural Journal*, vol. 9, no. 4, November, pp.243–9.

Discusses Practice Note 3 Root damage by trees; siting of dwellings and special precautions – published by the National House-Building Council Registration Council in 1969.

Bridgeman, P. (1979) *Trees for town and country: A practical guide to planting and care.* Newton Abbot: David and Charles. 144pp. (ISBN 0715378414).

Advises on the selection, planting and maintenance of the young tree, and lists the most suitable and attractive species for a variety of purposes and conditions. Other sections concern tree inspections, recognition of diseases, pruning, surgery and felling, with reference to the importance of trees on construction sites.

Browell, M. and Mead, H. (1987) 'Tree shelters', *Landscape Design*, April, pp.57–60.

Investigates the practical aspects of tree shelters designed to protect trees and shrubs from damage, to create a sheltered microclimate and to provide rapid establishment.

Clouston, B. and Stansfield, K. (eds.) (1981) *Trees in towns.* Architectural Press. 168pp. (ISBN 0851396585).

Discusses the importance of trees as visual elements in the townscape and provides advice on tree maintenance and care and repair of urban trees. Covers damage to foundations and drains caused by trees.

Davies, R.J. (1987) *Trees and weeds: weed control for successful tree establishment.* London: HMSO. Forestry Commission Handbook no. 2. 36pp. (ISBN 0117102083).

Looks at ways weeds can influence young trees and then discusses various methods of weed control.

Design guidelines trees: landscape design, planting and care (1985) London Borough of Richmond upon Thames. Leaflet.

Briefly describes enclosure, screen, planting, formal and informal planting, specimen planting, tree selection, site requirements, pruning and thinning.

Forestry Commission (1985) *Tree planting in colliery spoil.* By J. Jobling and R. Carnell. Edinburgh R&D Paper 136. (ISBN 0855381876).

Forestry Commission (1986) *Tree shelters: A guide to their use and information on suppliers.* prepared by Colin Shanks. Edinburgh. Spring. 7pp.

Offers advice on planting, weed control, stakes, erecting shelters, plastics and fastening methods, causes of failure and removal of shelters and ties.

Foster, R. (1982) *Trees and shrubs in garden design.* Newton Abbot: David and Charles. 231pp. (ISBN 0715382713).

Covers planting, care and cultivation, specimen trees and grouping of trees for maximum effect.

Gruffydd, D. *Tree form, size and colour: a guide to selection, planting and design.* London: Spon. 243pp. (ISBN 0419135200).

Includes guidance on design requirements, tree character, siting and display, light reflection, surface pattern, growth rate, atmospheric tolerance and planting distances.

Hillier, H.G. (1981) *Manual of trees and shrubs.* 5th rev. edn. Newton Abbot: David and Charles. 575pp. (ISBN 0715383027).

Provides descriptive and illustrative information on over 3500 woody plants.

Jaffa, G. (1984) 'Early recognition of tree disease', *Parks and Sports Grounds*, vol. 49, no. 7 April, pp.10–11.

Explains the difficulties in detecting disease in trees.

Littlewood, M. (1988) *Tree detailing.* London: Butterworth. 213pp. (ISBN 0408500026).

Covers stock, planting, pruning and surgery, protection of new trees and existing trees, tree surrounds, trees in containers, and roof gardens, maintenance and management, tree survey and evaluation.

Low, A.J. (1986) *Use of broadleaved species in upland forests – selection and establishment for environmental improvement.* London: HMSO. Forestry Commission Leaflet no. 88. 21pp.

Gives guidance on how best to select and establish broadleaved tree species for conservation, amenity and landscape purposes within upland coniferous forest areas of Great Britain.

Mitchell, A. and Jobling, J. (1984) *Decorative trees for country, town and garden.* London: HMSO. 146pp. (ISBN 0117100382).

Gives a visual aid to tree selection followed by sections on broadleaves and conifers. Details on features, merits, limitations, origins and cultivars are given for each species.

Mitchell, Alan (1985) 'Trees for towns and cities', *Arboricultural Journal*, November, pp.271–8.

Selection of trees for streets and restricted space.

Packham, R. and Bell, S. (1987) *Trees and the landowner*. Country Landowners Association. 30pp.

Looks at the law on preservation and felling of trees, forestry policy, procedure and grants.

Patch, D. (ed.) (1987) *Advances in practical arboriculture*. Proceedings of a seminar held at the University of York, 10–12 April 1985. London: HMSO Forestry Commission Bulletin no. 65. 196pp. (ISBN 0117102032).

Sections include: plant production; tree establishment; the mature tree and protection.

Patch, D. (1978) *Tree staking*. Farnham, Surrey: Arboriculture Advisory and Information Service. Arboriculture Research Note 40/87/ARB. 4pp.

Looks at reasons for and effects of staking. Also looks at minimizing the need for staking and treatment of previously staked trees.

Pepper, H.W., Rowe, J.J. and Tee, L.A. (1985) *Individual tree protection*. London: HMSO Forestry Commission Arboricultural Leaflet no. 10. 22pp.

Reviews the design requirements of individual tree protection and the ways in which these may be met in both the urban and rural environments.

Pepper, H.W. (1987) *Plastic mesh tree guards*. Farnham, Surrey: Arboriculture Advisory and Information Service Arboriculture Research Note 05/87/WILD. 9pp.

Describes light-degradable polyethylene plastic mesh tubes for use as tree guards to protect trees vulnerable to damage by rabbit or deer. Considers their use in towns.

Reader's Digest (1981) *Field guide to the trees and shrubs of Britain*. London. 303pp. (ISBN 0276002180).

Provides recognition profiles of more than 200 trees and shrubs, including all the species which grow wild in Britain and a wide selection of species introduced for garden and parkland planting.

Tabbish, P.M. (1986) *Rough handling reduces the viability of planting stock*. Farnham, Surrey: Forestry Commission Arboriculture Research Note 64/86/SILN. 2pp.

Thoday, P.R. (ed.) (1983) *Tree establishment*. Proceedings of the symposium held at the University of Bath on 14–15 July 1983. University of Bath. 78pp.

Covers amenity sites, planting, transplanting, establishing trees on damaged soils and tree roots.

Thomas, G.S. (1983) *Trees in the landscape*. London: Jonathan Cape. 200pp. (ISBN 022402051X).

Concerned with the artistic use of trees in landscaping.

Turfs and Lawns

see also BS 3969

Joint Council for Landscape Industries (1980) *Rules for measurement for soft landscape works.* Joint Council for Landscape Industries and British Association of Landscape Industries. 23pp.

Provides rules of measurement for cultivating and preparing ground, grass seeding and turfing, planting, thinning and pruning, tree surgery, grass improvement and aftercare of growing material.

Hubbard, C.E. (1985) *Grasses: a guide to their structure, identification, uses and distribution in the British Isles.* 3rd edn. Harmondsworth: Penguin Books. 476pp. (ISBN 0140222790).

Pycraft, D. (1980) *Lawns, ground cover and weed control: creating and maintaining a lawn, alternatives to grass, using ground cover plants, controlling weeds.* London: Mitchell Beazley. 96pp. (ISBN 0855332190). (Royal Horticultural Society's Encyclopaedia of Practical Gardening).

Contains practical information and diagrams.

Shildrick, J.P. (1988) *Amenity pesticides '87.* Bingley, W. Yorks: National Turfgrass Council. Workshop Report no. 12.

York, P. (1988) 'Essential irrigation', *Landscape Design*, December, pp.48–9.

Introduces the aims and objectives of the British Turf Irrigation Association and stresses that irrigation should be considered right from the start of landscape design.

Urban Landscape

Cartwright, R.W. (1980) *The design of urban space: A GLC manual.* Greater London Council Architectural Press. 163pp. (ISBN 0851396933).

Provides practical guidance in the form of drawings, dimensional data, and comparative tables of costs on the equipping and furnishing of roads, pedestrian areas, cycle paths, subways, play areas, sign systems, lighting and other public facilities.

Cullen, G. (1971) *The concise townscape.* London: Architectural Press. 198pp. (ISBN 0851395686).

Illustrations show the jumble of buildings, streets and spaces which make up the urban environment and explore the visual effects which can be created.

Department of the Environment (1987) *Greening city sites: Good practice in urban regeneration.* London: HMSO. 127pp. (ISBN 0117520130).

Discusses individual projects on recreation, housing related improvements, visual enhancements, industrial and commercial areas.

Downing, M.F. (1977) *Landscape construction.* London: Spon. 247pp. (ISBN 0419108904).

Intended as an introduction to techniques and methods for the student landscape architect and covers such topics as site investigation, drainage and water features.

Dutton, R.A. and Bradshaw, A.D. *Land reclamation in cities.* London: HMSO. (ISBN 0117515604).

Explains ways in which grass, shrubs and trees can be established temporarily or permanently on urban wasteland.

Gage, M. and Vandenberg, M. (1975) *Hard landscape in concrete.* London: Architectural Press. (ISBN 0851392776).

Discusses the general problem of urban design with reference to the use of land surfaces in the formation of urban spaces. Covers the pedestrian and vehicle environment, street furniture and play areas. Information sheets give guidance on how to achieve desired finishes.

Steels, H.M. and Haigh, R. (1988) 'Looking at landfill', *Landscape Design,* December pp.50–4.

Describes how the 27 million tonnes of waste created in Cheshire is put to practical use by the local authority.

Tandy, C. (ed.) (1978) *Handbook of urban landscape.* London: Architectural Press. 275pp. (ISBN 0851396917).

Comprehensive coverage of the design procedure, surveys, plant data, parks, open spaces, recreation, gardens, housing estates, elements of landscape construction.

Taylor, L. (ed.) (1981) *Urban open spaces.* London: Academy Editions. 128pp.

Examines the importance of open spaces to the urban environment and how to protect and renew them. Applies to parks, plazas, playgrounds, streets, gardens, rooftops and waterfronts.

Walls

see also Fences, Hedges and Shelterbelts

Aldridge, T.M. (1986) *Boundaries, walls and fences.* London: Longman. 6th edn. 66pp. (ISBN 0851212344).

Brings together the various rules and laws relating to boundaries of private properties, as currently in force.

British Trust for Conservation Volunteers (1978) *Dry stone walling: A practical conservation handbook.* London. 120pp. (ISBN 0950164356).

Covers walls in the landscape, conservation of dry stone walls, law, safety equipment and organization, construction techniques and types of stone.

Garner, L. (1985) *Dry stone walls.* Aylesbury, Bucks: Shire Publications 32pp. (ISBN 0852636660).

Describes how to build, repair and maintain dry stone walls.

Korff, J.O.A. (1984) *Design of freestanding walls.* Brick Development Association. 35pp.

Guidance for civil and structural engineers, architects and builders to the design and use of plain and reinforced freestanding brick walls not forming part of a building.

Littlewood, M. (1984) *Landscape detailing.* Architectural Press. 152pp. (ISBN 0851398596).

Comprises 13 sections ranging from freestanding walls to fences and gates, steps and ramps, drainage channels and tree surrounds. Each section begins with technical guidance notes on design and specification (including a list of relevant British Standards).

Water in the Landscape

Campbell, C.S. (1978) *Water in landscape architecture.* London: Van Nostrand Reinhold. 128pp. (ISBN 1442214596).

Deals with the technicalities and aesthetics of fountain design. The art of design is put in an historical perspective. Outlines basic principles of hydraulics; practical limitations; environment; available equipment. A large section examines recent water features around the world.

Eachus Huckson Partnership and Shaw, F. (1988) *The water industry in the countryside.* Cheltenham, Glos.: Countryside Commission. CCP 239. (ISBN 0861701682).

Offers guidance on conservation principles, public access and recreation, general water treatment to water authorities and all others concerned and interested in water and the land.

Jellicoe, S. and Jellicoe, G. (1971) *Water: the use of water in landscape architecture.* Adam and Charles Black. 137pp. (ISBN 071361188X).

Extensively illustrated. Considers the nature of water; water in use; the philosophy of water; water landscapes of the past, present and future.

Robinette, G.O. (1984) *Water conservation in landscape design and management.* London: Van Nostrand Reinhold. 258pp. (ISBN 0442222041).

Covers all aspects of monitoring water usage, redesigning landscapes to use less water and applying water to plants in the most efficient way possible.

Travers Morgan (1987) *Changing river landscapes.* Cheltenham, Glos.: Countryside Commission. CCP 238. (ISBN 0861701615).

Assesses land use and landscape changes and their long term impact.

Wyson, A (1986) *Aquatecture: architecture and water.* London: Architectural Press. 216pp. (ISBN 0851397271).

Traces the history of the relationship between architecture and water, illustrates examples and gives practical advice on man-made landscape and water.

Woodlands

Crowther, R.E. and Evans, J. (1986) *Coppice.* 2nd edn. London: HMSO. Forestry Commission Leaflet no 83. 23pp.

Provides practical, managerial and silvicultural information for all those involved in coppice woodlands.

Evans, J. (1984) *Silviculture of broadleaved woodland.* London: HMSO. Forestry Commission Bulletin no 62. 232pp.

Describes silvicultural practices appropriate to a wide range of woodland types and conditions.

Managing small woodlands. (1980) Cheltenham, Glos.: Countryside Commission. Leaflet no. 6. (ISBN 0902590960).

Peterken, G.F. (1981) *Woodland conservation and management.* London: Chapman Hall. 328pp. (ISBN 0412128209).

Describes the origins, management and ecological characteristics of British woodlands. Shows how forestry and conservation can work in unison.

Small woods on farms. (1983) Cheltenham, Glos.: Countryside Commission. CCP 143. (ISBN 086170035X).

The Dartington Amenity Research Trust studied small woods in nine areas of England and Wales. Their report suggests ways of ensuring the future of these woods in the landscape, including management for timber as well as conservation and recreation.

British Standards

BS 187 : 1978 *Specification for calcium silicate (sandlime and flintlime) bricks.* Amendment no. 1 1987. BSI, 1978. 16pp.

BS 340 : 1979 *Specification for precast concrete kerbs, channels, edgings and quadrants.* BSI, 1979. 12.pp.

BS 497 : Part 1 : 1976 *Cast iron and cast steel.* BSI, 1976. 12pp.

BS 594 : Part 1 : 1985 *Hot-rolled asphalt for roads and other paved areas.* Part 1: Specification for constituent materials and asphalt mixtures. BSI, 1985. 15pp.

Specifies requirements for hot-rolled asphalt as laid as wearing course base course or roadbase for roads and over-paved areas. Includes guidance on selection of asphalt mixtures and their ingredients.

BS 873 : Part 6 : 1983 *Specification for retroreflective and non-retroreflective signs.* BSI, 1983. 12pp.

General constructional requirements for sign plates, frames and fittings, together with the photometric, colorimetric and performance requirements.

BS 873 : Part 1 : 1983 *Road traffic signs and internationally illuminated bollards.* Methods of test. BSI, 1983. 20pp.

Describes general test procedures for signs and bollards, including photometric tests, general strength tests and tests for assessing resistance to weathering and corrosion.

BS 873 : Part 3: 1980 *Specification for internally illuminated bollards.* BSI, 1980. 12pp.

Requirements for the design and performance of internally illuminated bollards excluding spring-back bollards.

BS 873 : Part 5 : 1983 *Specification for internally illuminated signs and external lighting luminaires.* BSI, 1983. 12pp.

General constructional requirements for signs incorporating a means of illumination, including requirements for electrical safety and light sources. Limits for the mean luminance and uniformity of luminance on the sign face are specified.

BS 881 and 589 : 1974 *Nomenclature of commercial timbers, including sources of supply.* BSI, 1974. 87pp.

BS 882 : 1983 *Specification for aggregates from natural sources for concrete.* Amendment no. 1, 1986. BSI, 1983. 12pp.

BS 1192 : Part 4 : 1984 *Recommendations for landscape drawings.* BSI, 1984. 40pp.

Includes symbols and abbreviations which are used in a series of typical drawings. Appendices include summaries of information commonly used when landscape drawings are being prepared.

BS 1147 : 1988 *Specification for mastic asphalt (limestone fine aggregate) for roads and footways.* BSI, 1988. 8pp.

BS 1722 : Part 2 : 1973 *Woven wire fences.* Amendment no. 1, 1976. BSI, 1973. 28pp.
BS 1722 : Part 3 : 1986 *Specification for strained wire fences.* BSI, 1986. 28pp.
BS 1722 : Part 4 : 1986 *Specification for cleft chestnut pale fences.* BSI, 1986. 12pp.
BS 1722 : Part 5 : 1986 *Specification for close boarded fences.*
BS 1722 : Part 6 : 1986 *Specification for wooden palisade fences.* BSI, 1986. 24pp.
BS 1722 : Part 7 : 1986 *Specification for wooden post and rail fences.* BSI, 1986. 16pp.
BS 1722 Part 8 : 1978 *Mild steel (low carbon steel) continuous bar fences.* BSI, 1978, 8pp.

BS 1722 : Part 9 : 1979 *Mild steel (low carbon steel) fences with round or square verticals and flat posts and horizontals.* BSI, 1979. 8pp.

BS 1722 : Part 11 : 1986 *Specification for woven wood and lap boarded panel fences.* BSI, 1986. 24pp.

BS 1722 : Part 12 : 1979 *Steel palisade fences.* BSI, 1979. 12pp.

BS 3882 : 1965 *Recommendations and classification for topsoil.* BSI, 1965. 9pp. Amd. 3089, no. 1, 1979.

Description of topsoil; classification by texture, pH., stone content. Notes on method of test for topsoil.

BS 3921 : 1985 *Specification for clay bricks.* BSI, 1985. 24pp.

BS 3936 : Part 1 : 1980 *Nursery stock: Specification for trees and shrubs.* BSI, 1980. 12pp.

Trees and shrubs, including conifers and woody climbing plants, suitable to be transplanted and grown for amenity. Covers origin, root system, condition, dimensions, packaging and labelling, and forms and sizes to be supplied for a wide range of species.

BS 3936 : Part 4 : 1984 *Specification for forest trees.* BSI, 1984. 8pp.

BS 3969 : 1965 (1978) *Recommendations for turf for general landscape purposes.* BSI, 1978. 8pp.

Provides details of desirable and undesirable grasses and weeds, soil, condition and dimensions of turves.

BS 3975 : Part 4 : 1966 *Plant description.* BSI, 1966. 28pp.

BS 3875 : Part 5 : 1969 *Horticultural, arboricultural and forestry practice.* BSI, 1969. 48pp.

Provides working definitions for terms commonly used in nursery practice, horticultural upkeep and ground maintenance, tree work and forestry.

BS 3998 : 1966 *Recommendations for tree work.* BSI, 1966. 32pp.

Covers safety and equipment; individual operations; cuts, pruning; lifting of crown; thinning; reducing; reshaping; restoration; repair work; bracing; feeding; tree removal.

BS 4043 : 1966 (1978) *Recommendations for transplanting semi-mature trees.* BSI, 1978. 28pp.

Comprehensive details on suitable trees for transplanting, season by season. Tree pits, drainage, tree lifting operations. Guying and securing the tree, wrapping, watering and spraying.

BS 4428 : 1969 (1979) *Recommendations for general landscape operations (excluding hard surfaces).* BSI, 1969 (1979). 52pp. Amd. 938, 1972.

Deals with the following general landscape operations: preparatory operations, including earthwork, land shaping and drainage; seeding of grass areas;

turfing; planting of shrubs, hedges, climbers, herbaceous plants and bulbs; individual tree planting, forestry planting for amenity purposes.

BS 4987 *Coated macadam for roads and other paved areas.* BS 4987 : Part 1 : 1988 *Specification for constituent materials and for mixtures.* 25pp.

BS 4987 : Part 2 : 1988 *Specification for transport, laying and compaction.* 8pp.

BS 5236 : 1975 *Recommendations for cultivation and planting of trees in the advanced nursery stock category.* BSI, 1975. 12pp.

BS 5273 : 1975 *Dense tar surfacing for roads and other paved areas.* BSI, 1975. 7pp.

Specifies the composition, manufacture, testing and transport of dense tar surfacing as defined in BS 892.

BS 5390: 1976 (1984) *Code of practice for stone masonry.* 44pp. Amendment no. 1, 1983.

BS 5628 : Part 3 : 1985 *Materials and components, design and workmanship.* Amendment no. 1, 1985. BSI, 1985. 104pp.

BS 5696 *Plant equipment intended for permanent installation outdoors.*
BS 5696 : Part 1 : 1986 *Methods of test.* 16pp. Amendment no. 1, 1987.
BS 5696 : Part 2 : 1986 *Specification for construction and performance.* 20pp.
BS 5696 : Part 3 : 1979 *Code of practice for installation and maintenance.* 8pp. Amendment no. 1 1980.

BS 5837 : 1980 *Code of practice for trees in relation to construction.* BSI, 1980. 28pp.

Principles to follow to achieve satisfactory juxtaposition of trees and construction. Recommends types of trees for planting near buildings, structures, plant and services. Advice on planting and maintenance of trees in urban locations and paved areas.

BS 6073 : Part 1 : 1981 *Specification for precast concrete masonry units.* Amendment no. 1, 1982. Amendment no. 2, 1984. BSI, 1981. 16pp.

BS 6431 : Part 22 : 1986 *Ceramic floor and wall tiles: method for determination of frost resistance.* BSI, 1986. 12pp.

BS 6677 *Clay and calcium silicate pavers for flexible pavements.*
BS 6677 : Part 1 : 1986 *Specification for pavers,* 12pp.
BS 6677 : Part 2 : 1986 *Code of practice for design of lightly trafficked pavements,* 12pp.
BS 6677 : Part 3 : 1986 *Method for construction of pavements,* 8pp.

BS 6717 : Part 1 : 1986 *Precast concrete paving blocks: specification for paving blocks.* BSI, 1986. 8pp.

INDEX

PICTURE INDEX

Photographic and illustration credits for the figures

8.7   Ken Fieldhouse
8.8   Michael Oldham
8.9   Adrian Lisney

Chapter 9
Frontispiece   Patrick Charlton
9.1   Ken Fieldhouse
9.2   Michael Oldham
9.3   Michael Oldham
9.4   Patrick Charlton
9.5   Ken Fieldhouse
9.6   Michael Oldham
9.7   Michael Oldham

Chapter 10
Frontispiece   Michael Oldham
10.1   Patrick Charlton
10.2   Ken Fieldhouse
10.3   Ken Fieldhouse
10.4   Patrick Charlton

Chapter 11
Frontispiece   Michael Oldham
11.1   Patrick Charlton
11.2   Adrian Lisney
11.3   Adrian Lisney

Chapter 12
Frontispiece   Adrian Lisney
12.1   Michael Oldham
12.2   Ken Fieldhouse
12.3   Patrick Charlton
12.4   Patrick Charlton
12.5   Ken Fieldhouse

Chapter 13
Frontispiece   Ken Fieldhouse
13.1   Ken Fieldhouse
13.2   Adrian Lisney
13.3   Ken Fieldhouse

Chapter 14
Frontispiece   Michael Oldham
14.1   Michael Oldham
14.2   Julie Layzell
14.3   Maria Luczak

Chapter 15
Frontispiece   Adrian Lisney
15.1   Michael Oldham
15.2   Michael Oldham
15.3   Michael Oldham
15.4   Michael Oldham
15.5   Michael Ellison
15.6   Michael Oldham

Chapter 16
Frontispiece   Michael Oldham
16.1   Michael Oldham
16.2   Michael Oldham
16.3   Adrian Lisney
16.4   Michael Oldham
16.5   Patrick Charlton
16.6   Patrick Charlton
16.7   Adrian Lisney
16.8   Michael Oldham
16.9   Michael Oldham
16.10   Michael Oldham
16.11   Julie Layzell

Colour Section
Plate 1   Patrick Charlton
Plate 2   Michael Oldham
Plate 3   Patrick Charlton
Plate 4   Ken Fieldhouse
Plate 5   Ken Fieldhouse
Plate 6   Michael Ellison
Plate 7   Adrian Lisney
Plate 8   Patrick Charlton
Plate 9   Ken Fieldhouse
Plate 10   Ken Fieldhouse
Plate 11   Department of the Environment
Plate 12   Michael Ellison
Plate 13   Michael Oldham